a girl and her greens

A Girl and Her Pig

a girl and her greens
hearty meals from the garden

APRIL BLOOMFIELD
with JJ GOODE

photographs by david loftus

illustrations by sun young park

ecco

An Imprint of HarperCollins *Publishers*

HarperCollins books may be purchased for educational, business, or sales promotional use. For information please e-mail the Special Markets Department at SPsales@harpercollins.com.

FIRST EDITION

Designed by Suet Yee Chong

Library of Congress Cataloging-in-Publication Data has been applied for.

ISBN 978-0-06-222588-7

15 16 17 18 19   SCP   10 9 8 7 6 5 4 3

contents

acknowledgments

Let's start with the most important person: Thank you to Louis Russo, the young man who came up with the title for this book!

Thank you to the amazing team at Ecco, especially Dan Halpern, Gabriella Doob, Libby Edelson, Suet Chong, Allison Saltzman, and Rachel Meyers, for helping me create a book that I adore. And best of luck at your new job, Libby.

To my superstar agent, the always dapper Luke Janklow.

To my friend and cowriter, JJ Goode, for driving me nuts, making me measure, and making me laugh.

To my friend, the brilliant photographer David Loftus, and food and prop stylist Georgie ("Puddin' and Pie") Socratous and Irene Wong for helping me make this book beautiful.

To Sun Young Park for her incredible illustrations.

To my friend Martin Schoeller for yet another lovely cover photo.

To Amy Vogler and Marian Bull for their careful, thoughtful recipe testing.

To Jamie Oliver, Pete Begg, and Dolly Sweet for their advice, support, and friendship.

To my friend and partner Ken Friedman. When shall we open another one?

To my hardworking and patient assistant, SarahGlenn Bernstein.

To my wonderful staff, who kept everything humming away while I worked on this book. Special thanks to Katharine Marsh, Christina Lecki, Josh Even, Ryan Jordan, Amy Hess, Robert Flaherty, Charlene Santiago, Jimbo Gibson, Edie Ugot, and Peter Cho.

To Amy Hou, my rock.

introduction

I've developed a bit of a reputation for meat, particularly the odd parts—what I call the not-so-nasty bits. I certainly do adore trotters and kidneys and liver. I get chuffed about a roast dinner or sticky veal shank or a good burger. Yet lamb shoulders and suckling pigs are sort of like action films, with lots of explosions and excitement. You like them, but you probably don't want to watch them *all* the time. And not even the juiciest steak or crispiest pig's ear gets me happy like nice peas.

Just about my favorite thing to do is go to the farmers' market in spring in search of flawless pea pods, unblemished and full. I walk around like a kid in a sweet shop, nabbing a pod at my favorite stand, gently squeezing until it splits to reveal a happy row of peas, and popping one in my mouth. You know when you like something so much that it makes you not just nod your head in satisfaction, but shake your head in disbelief? That's what happens when I find that perfectly sweet pea. So many things conspired to make that pea—the weather, the soil, the farmer—and there you are on the receiving end. It makes me happy and grateful.

And I love that later on, I know I'll be propped up at the counter with my big bag of peas, gently squeezing their bottoms so the pods pop open, running my finger along each one to split them, and nudging the peas into a bowl, listening to the pitter-patter sound they make as they tumble in. If I ever get up the nerve to get a tattoo, I'll get one that shows a few pretty green pods.

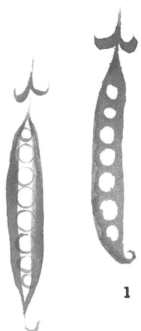

I didn't exactly grow up on a farm. I grew up in Birmingham, the second largest city in England and, like most big cities, one dominated by

1

concrete and shopping centers. I was as particular an eater then as I am today. While nowadays I get fussy about finding the sweetest peas and the prettiest carrots, back when I was little, I got fussy about liking my bacon sandwiches with the slices still a bit floppy and a good dose of HP sauce. I insisted on eating my fish stick sandwiches with butter and ketchup. When my nan skewered pineapple and cheddar chunks for a party, as people used to back then, I'd always steal the pineapple but leave the cheddar. To eat my Cadbury Flake, I'd squeeze the long package to crumble up the chocolate, then I'd open one side and tip it all into my mouth at once.

Like many working-class people, my parents didn't always have time to shop for fresh vegetables, let alone peel them. I ate plenty of cauliflower, broccoli, and carrots that came from freezer bags. I'd cram these horrible veg into my cheeks like a chipmunk does, because I knew I had to eat them but I wanted to delay the chewing and the tasting. Frozen peas, however, I loved. I still do.

When the vegetables were fresh, they were often cooked in the English manner of the times—that is, for too long, until they were squishy and a little gray. I still remember some godawful Brussels sprouts, which at the time I just loved, boiled to buggery in a pressure cooker. England has come a long way since then.

We'd occasionally eat marrow, a sort of watery, overgrown zucchini, as big as my forearm. My mom would scrape out the seedy middles to make canoes, pack in minced meat, and bake them. I quite liked these, the way the marrow got creamy and you could just shovel it into your mouth with the meat without thinking that you were eating the vegetable. For a spell in the '80s, after we moved house and got our first microwave, my family lived on potatoes "baked" in the futuristic oven. Imagine, putting something as lovely as a potato in the microwave! Even as a girl, I knew how wonderful potatoes could be, thanks to my school's cafeteria. I might have been horrible at my times tables—while the rest of the class was on 6s, I could barely make it through my 2s—but I was quite good at eating steamy boiled potatoes bombarded with butter and black pepper.

My early vegetable mentors weren't chefs obsessed with the perfect tomato or blokes who plunged their hands into the cool dirt to pull up carrots. One of them was my granddad. When I was a girl, he ran a small café called Lincon Road. His customers were a mix of Mods and Rockers. Mods wore suits with thin ties, rode mopeds, and listened to dub music and The Who; Rockers wore leather, rode proper motorcycles, and listened to Elvis and Eddie Cochrane. When the two factions weren't fighting each other, they were trying to drill a hole in the café's pinball machine to get at the coins inside. My granddad tried to keep the peace with tea and toast.

He loved his café. And he was a good cook. He was particularly proud of the fry-ups he cooked there, which along with the mandatory egg, bread, sausage, and bacon included lowly vegetables like button mushrooms, Heinz tinned baked beans, and pale tomato halves browned slightly in hot fat. While I loved the meaty bits, I had special affection for those tomatoes. Just when you thought you couldn't take another bite of sausage, the tomatoes' acidity would revive your palate and you'd go back in for more.

My nan, who passed away more than a decade ago, also put thought and attention into her vegetable cookery. She made the best Sunday roast, which was less about the lamb or pork she made than it was about the unromantic array of carrots, parsnips, peas, sprouts, potatoes, and swedes—that is, rutabagas to you Yanks out there— none of the Treviso, ramps, and Romanesco that get me giddy these days. The pile on my plate, so high it nearly reached my chin, was mostly veg. She was really good with mise en place: growing up, I delighted in visiting her house and seeing the stove arranged with little pots, each filled with peeled vegetables ready to be cooked.

My mom might not have been the world's greatest cook, but she did have a little garden. My parents didn't have much money, but they were quite house-proud and always kept our modest row house in Druid's Heath looking nice. In the backyard, my mom planted pretty little plots of pansies and strawberries,

tomatoes, and spring onions. I loved the taste of her tomatoes straight off the vine, though when she made salad with those same tomatoes and her spring onions, I'd still douse the whole thing with Heinz Salad Cream, like a proper kid. I wish everyone had their own garden. I wish I had my own garden. In New York City, I don't even have a pot on the fire escape.

Things changed after I finished my first cooking job, at the carvery station at a Holiday Inn. I was lucky to work for chefs with an affection for produce, like Rowley Leigh and Simon Hopkinson. But my own affection for veg really took off when I started at The River Café, working for Rose Gray and Ruth Rogers.

I was swept up by all of their obsessions, especially the vegetables that they sourced from Italy. There were proper Florence fennel and artichokes and celeriac that Rose and Ruth brought in by the pallet. Until then, these were things I liked all right but didn't really understand. I knew celeriac to be a pleasant, if unremarkable, root whose main distinction was that it was knobby, and a bit homely. Not at The River Café. There it was dense and sweet. A sniff at the base would yield that floral aroma, just as it would when I sniffed a ripe melon.

Besides rediscovering old friends, I also met new ones, like the Roman delicacy called puntarelle, a highly seasonal chicory whose slender leaves are very, very bitter. Because Rose and Ruth adored it, I ate it again and again in order to understand the pleasure they took in it, in the same way you want to try lager because your dad drinks it, then next thing you know you see past the bitterness and actually enjoy it yourself.

After five years at The River Café, I moved to Berkeley, California. The first day I arrived at my flat on Shattuck and Folsom, I was too chuffed to just sit around, so I dropped my bags and had a wander. I didn't know my way, but next thing I knew, I was staring at a big peace sign made out of garlic heads hanging on a gate outside a restaurant. I had stumbled on Chez Panisse, where I had come to work. My new boss was Chris Lee, and his kitchen was filled with people who had been cooking there for ten years. That told me a lot about the place, straight away. Jobs in restaurant kitchens are typically high-turnover, because of the intensity of the work, the low pay, and cranky-knickers bosses like yours truly; but there, no one seemed to ever want to leave.

Chez Panisse, if you haven't heard, was a pioneer in simple, ingredient-driven cooking. Working there, you couldn't help but develop a close connection to the ingredients at hand. In fact, part of the job was learning how they were grown. That's how I came to visit Green String Farm (then called Cannard Farm) in Sonoma County, which supplied much of the produce we cooked with at Chez Panisse. I met an engaging man called Bob Cannard, who taught me how much work and passion it takes to grow wonderful vegetables. I learned that not all soil is created equal and that you could alter its mineral composition (Bob enriched it with pulverized oyster shells, old crops left to die, and something he called "compost tea") to give the vegetables what they needed to grow and be tasty. I learned that bugs weren't necessarily the enemies of veg-etables. Bob considered bugs to be helpful little critters—seeing them ravaging a plant told him that the plant itself wasn't healthy enough to ward off the fellows. It's funny, but toiling in a windowless restaurant kitchen, it's surprisingly easy to forget that vegetables come from seeds in the ground and not from boxes brought by your purveyor.

I might never have left California with its vast variety of produce, available almost all year round, if I hadn't been offered the job at The Spotted Pig. I'm happy I did leave, if only because I like the East Coast and its more dramatic seasons. Every time you turn around, there's

something new to be excited about: Ooh, ramps are coming in! Fantastic, pumpkin is back!

One of the loveliest things about vegetables is their ability to evoke a particular season or place. Meat and seafood can do this, too—there's spring lamb, softshell crabs, and shad roe—but nothing like how a heap of ramps at the farmers' market announces spring's arrival or how endless punnets of tomatoes on a table at a farmstand signal summer. When the leaves begin to turn, you won't spot eggplants at the market. When you're still wearing your thermals, you won't find spring garlic, with their purple-speckled bulbs and pert green stalks, no matter how hard you search. And that's OK. In fact, I quite like it.

Life would be boring if you could have everything at any time. I like the limits that the seasons impose. I like having something to look forward to. I don't even mind when nature disappoints me with a bad year for corn or tomatoes. You develop an almanac in your head—like, "Oh, tomatoes were so bad that year." When great ones return, you get to think, "Finally, lovely tomatoes!" Vegetables make you happy when they're there, and you miss them when they're gone.

When I told a friend that I was working on a vegetable cookbook, he said that this made sense, since vegetables have become so trendy. I had a good laugh at that. I guess I must have lost the plot somewhere along the way, because I still don't think beets, carrots, and asparagus are cool. I do, however, think that they're delicious. That's good enough for me.

But I suppose I see what my mate meant. Lately, you've got people like Michael Pollan and Mark Bittman making the case with science and common sense that we should all cut back on meat, for our health as well as for the planet's. Chefs have been taking up the cause, treating veg with the love and care once reserved mainly for rib eye steaks and lamb chops. My motivation is more about passion than scruples. I'm not trying to make a statement. I just love the way boiled broccoli raab sort of bites the back of your mouth. I love how creamy properly cooked eggplant gets. I could shuck corn all day, thinking about how sweet it'll taste.

Vegetables have some practical advantages over meat, too. For example, while pork shoulders and legs of lamb need to be cooked softly, you're not going to braise an artichoke for hours. Still, I don't like to think of cooking, eating, and enjoying vegetables as something you do while you're not eating meat. While this book is about vegetables, not all the recipes are vegetarian. I like cooking my collards with lots of bacon. Anchovies give so many veg a lift. Some vegetables even turn meaty on you. Red onion gives sauces and soups a meatiness that other onions don't. Mushrooms give off an inviting aroma as they sear, which makes me think of veal kidneys. Artichoke hearts have a fleshy texture. Boiled asparagus can be juicy. I'm not saying vegetables should aspire to be like meat. I'm just saying that meat eaters will appreciate these qualities, and that vegetables *can* satisfy you the way meat does.

the farmers' market

Before you cook, you must shop, and there's no better place to shop than the farmers' market. Your goal is to find the best vegetables that you can. The higher your standards, the better your food will be.

First off, have a brisk walk through the market without buying a thing. This is especially true for markets that are new to you, where you don't know the vendors well. Because while it's tempting to jump at the first bunch of radishes you spot, not all veg, no matter how lovingly they're grown, are the same. What a shame it would be to buy radishes at one stand only to come across even perter, more peppery ones elsewhere. You want to make your walk brisk—really get a wiggle on!—so you can get back to any bunches and baskets that struck you earlier, before they get snapped up.

If you have the opportunity to taste what you see, please do, though you should ask your farmer nicely first. Taste everything you can. In the summer, taste cherry tomatoes until you find those that are thrillingly sweet-tart and explode when you bite them. In the spring, taste peas. I like to visit every stand and ogle the bins of peas, looking for the prettiest ones. Then I'll pick out a nice plump pod and pinch it open. Pop a pea in your mouth. If it's candy sweet and barely starchy, grab a bag and fill it up. Taste arugula from this stand and that until you find the one that aggressively bites the sides of your tongue.

Have a chat with a farmer. You might learn that her pumpkins are especially sweet thanks in part to a frost upstate. She might turn you on to an oddball mushroom that she tells you tastes a bit like crab, or you might encounter so-called over-wintered broccoli raab, which is especially sweet. And don't forgot to snap pictures of celebrity vegeta-

bles, such as the hard-to-find Rosa Bianca variety of eggplant (squat and ridged with mottled light purple and white skin), so you can look at them during a dull moment in your day or while planning a dinner, and get reinvigorated.

It should go without saying that you should never pick anything that's bruised, spongy, or bendy. But perfect-looking vegetables don't always taste perfect. Selecting great vegetables comes with experience. When you taste something at the market, or later as you're cooking, take a close look at it. Wonder what was it about this zucchini—perhaps it was a big honking thing—that might have warned you that it would taste so bland. What was it about this tomato—perhaps it was evenly colored, even near the stem, and heavy for its size—that could have told you it would be so sweet and meaty?

This way, you'll develop preferences. One of my preferences, in general, is for small to medium-size vegetables. I don't care for spindly, sprouty asparagus, but I'm not into fat stalks either. Tiny zucchini are

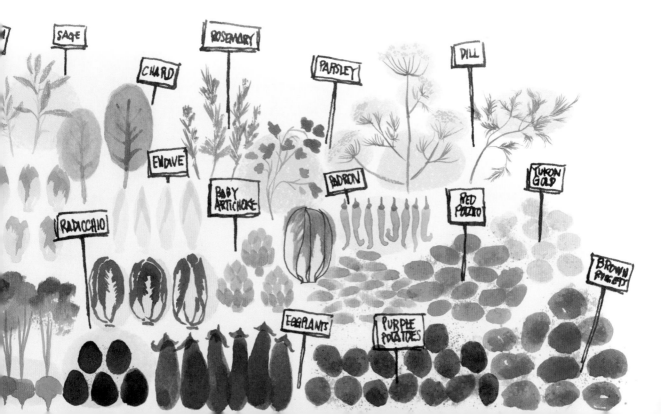

adorable, but so small that you don't get to enjoy the vegetable's character. I could live without baby fennel, which is too small to serve as crunchy slices or to be boiled to a creamy, meaty texture. Large pea pods seem tempting until you realize that the biggest ones tend to be starchy. While you might be tempted by a massive carrot, thinking you'd only have to peel that one, keep in mind that smaller carrots tend to taste sweeter and have thin skin that you don't need to peel at all.

Certain vegetables need to be used as soon as possible. Peas, corn, and green beans are sweetest just after they're picked. As they sit, the sugars turn to starch. So when you find sweet corn at the market, cook it for dinner that night.

Of course, vegetables don't always cooperate. Then you must adapt. If you'd like to make salad but the tomatoes are nearly bursting from the skins, consider making sauce instead. If you can't find tomatoes that meet your standard, change your plans on what to cook for dinner. You never want to go to the market stubborn.

the simple things

Often I find that the least exciting way of cooking actually leads to the most wonderful place. In fact, I like lots of vegetables—artichokes, Brussels sprouts, cauliflower—just boiled in salty water and served with a glug of olive oil and a sprinkle of chile or a tender squeeze of lemon. If you've got perfect veg, there's no need to manipulate it. There's nothing wrong with finding broccoli raab and just blanching it. Maybe you're thinking, "Blanched broccoli, that sounds like the worst thing in the world." But if your product is amazing and you don't cook it to buggery, then just blanching it can be the most beautiful thing.

In fact, part of me thinks that unless you're a practiced home cook, you should treat all vegetables like this, though a list of stuff I like to boil wouldn't make for much of a cookbook, now would it? Nor would it go over well at my restaurants if I served only plates of boiled swede and boiled carrots. That's why in this cookbook most of the recipes go much further than plain old boiling.

Yet because the simplest preparations deserve attention as well, I've sprinkled throughout the book a handful of not quite recipes for some of my favorite vegetables. I wanted to share with you the way I eat ingredients like tomatoes, corn, and potatoes at home, when I don't have to please anyone but myself. They're so simple that they don't require full-on recipes. Instead, they're more like little road maps encouraging you to play around and find your own way. Whatever you do, you want your potatoes to still taste like potatoes, your corn to still taste like corn. Whatever you add—lemon, chile, anchovy, or all three—shouldn't dominate. These kinds of flavor enhancers should help bring out the good qualities of the veg or serve to balance its harsh ones.

My hope is that you'll start playing with vegetables on your own. Take fennel, lovely fennel. When it's raw, it has a soft crunch and subtle anise-y sweetness. When you boil the fennel, its texture goes creamy and its sweetness really comes out to say hello. You don't *have to* do anything more but sometimes it's good fun to continue to transform the flavor, though never so much that you obscure the essence of the fennel itself. Maybe you decide to go that extra step and concentrate that sweetness by sautéing the boiled fennel, then balancing that sweetness with a little acidity—a splash of vinegar or tart citrus. If you're feeling ambitious, you might start exploring different sides of the same vegetable, combining raw and roasted fennel.

Never neglect the simple pleasures of cooking. When recipes do require more than a dunk in boiling water, try not to look at the process as a chore. If you think about how slow-cooked onions will ultimately transform a dish, the work itself becomes exciting. Get to know the process. Many of my recipes begin the same way, with onions and perhaps garlic or carrots sweating in hot fat. Settle in at the stove while they sizzle. Stir them and watch closely as they change. As you stir, look out for the point they begin to stick to the pan ever so slightly, which happens right before browning begins. Taste them, so you can see how sweet they're becoming. Have a good old sniff. These are the little pleasures of cooking, the gifts a cook gets in return for making dinner. And attention to these details is what makes food taste wonderful. When garlic goes toasty and golden, it unleashes umami and colors the entire dish with its warm, nutty flavor. Onions can become incredibly sweet, leaking that sweetness into stews and sauces. The way you treat onions and garlic, even though the two are not usually the starring veg, determines the character of the final dish. Browning them will make the entire dish taste hearty, more appropriate for a chilly day. Lowering the heat and keeping them free of color makes for a lighter tasting dish, even when it features a hefty veg like parsnips or cauliflower. Rush the process, however, and your food will lack depth. Get distracted and your garlic will burn.

I hope you'll keep this in mind as you read my recipes. As I did in my first cookbook, I decided that instead of writing recipes that look invitingly short, I'd offer recipes full of the little details that make food great. So please don't mistake a recipe that looks long for a recipe that's too complex to cook.

be fussy

Once you get to cooking, you should be particular, or to be less charitable, fussy, about the ingredients you use. That the tastier these raw ingredients are the better your food will be should go without saying.

Yet while I reckon that everyone agrees that a sweet pea is more delicious than a starchy bland one, I also reckon that each cook has her own quirky preferences. I embrace mine, which is why the recipes in this book are the way they are.

I leave the skin and spindly roots on beets, because they're tasty and pretty. I often blanch and peel tomatoes that I plan to cook with, sometimes even running the result through a food mill to achieve a smooth texture, without bothersome bits of seeds. I always peel the caps of portobello mushrooms, though I'm not quite sure why.

I'm particular, too, about some of the ingredients that many recipes in this book share. Here, you'll find a rundown of these staple ingredients that reflects my quirks. I hope you'll try things my way, but I know the way you cook is a reflection of who you are and everyone's different. Whether you adopt my eccentricities or not, you too should embrace your inner fuss-bucket and decide what you like and what gets you grumpy.

ANCHOVIES

Anchovies are good friends to vegetables, adding salty umami but not necessarily fishy flavor. I prefer salt-packed whole anchovies to oil-packed fillets. You'll need to fillet them yourself, but it only takes a few extra minutes. If you must use the oil-packed kind, make sure they're top quality—I like the Ortiz brand—and that you gently wipe the oil from the fillets before you cook with them.

Soaking and filleting salt-packed anchovies

Rinse the anchovies one at a time under cold running water, rubbing them gently between your fingers to remove the salt. Put them in a small bowl and add just enough water to cover. After about a minute—if you soak them for too long, they'll lose their umami quality—give them another quick rinse.

To fillet the anchovies, hold an anchovy under cold running water. Use your fingers to brush away the soft, loose matter near the head and at the belly. Rub the outside to remove any remaining salt or hard bits. Keeping the anchovy under the water, gently work a fingertip along the belly to start to separate the fillets. Gently pull the fillets apart—this should be easy, especially once you get the hang of it. Drape the now boneless fillet over the edge of a bowl to drain. Take the second fillet and pinch the backbone, pull it gently out, and discard it. Put the second fillet next to the first. Do the same with the rest of the anchovies.

GARLIC

In this book, I call for two types of garlic: standard garlic and spring garlic. By the time you buy standard garlic, the bulbs have hung in a warm, dry place for several weeks until the skins dry out and become papery. The process, known as "curing," helps preserve the garlic. Spring garlic, however, is eaten right after it's pulled from the earth, and has a sweeter, milder flavor. During its season, I often use spring garlic in place of standard garlic, though I add a bit more since its flavor is not as strong. The standard garlic you get at farmers' markets is typically good and fresh. At many grocery stores, however, it often has a little bright green germ growing inside or even peeking out the tip of the cloves. If you're fussy like me, you'll slice garlic cloves in half lengthwise and flick this green bit out before you get to chopping or cooking. Some people say the green bit makes your food a bit bitter; I don't find it bitter, but have seen it contribute an off-putting blue-ish color to what I'm cooking.

HERBS

Herbs are delicate things. When you're washing and handling them, be gentle. With herbs like basil and mint, which oxidize easily, be especially careful and always chop or tear them just before you plan to use them. Because herbs are so fragile, I'm always torn about how to pro-

vide measurements for them. I hate the idea of calling for tablespoons and cups, because thinking about someone cramming delicate herbs in a cup measure makes my bum cheeks clench. So I've opted for measurements that feel more natural to me: handfuls, small handfuls, and what I call five-finger pinches. Imagine a heap of mint leaves—a five-finger pinch means as much as you can grab with just the tips of all five fingers, as opposed to a typical pinch for which you'd grab with just your thumb and two fingers. Most of these measurements assume that you've picked the leaves from the tough stems. For parsley and cilantro, however, I like to use what I call "delicate sprigs," which are a few inches long and include thin, tender stems as well as leaves.

TOMATOES

I'm plenty fussy about tomatoes, whether they're fresh or canned. I often treat both to a little grooming before I cook with them.

Peeling fresh tomatoes

In several recipes, I call for tomatoes to be peeled. Here's how to do it: Bring a large pot of water to a boil. Use a knife to cut a shallow "X" at the bottom of each tomato. Working in batches of tomatoes of similar size, carefully plunge them in the boiling water and blanch for 20 seconds for larger tomatoes, and about 10 seconds for smaller ones. Gently transfer them to a colander and run them under cold running water. The peels will have loosened and you should be able to pull them off easily at the "X."

Draining and trimming canned tomatoes

Any recipe in this book that calls for canned tomatoes asks that you drain and trim them. First, drain and discard the liquid they come in, which I find tastes artificially sweet and salty. Second, trim any yellowish patches, straggling skin, and the tough core from each tomato.

put a spring
in your step

CRUSHED SPRING PEAS WITH MINT

As a girl in England, I always loved mushy peas, whether they were made the real way—from a starchy variety of pea called marrowfat that's dried, then soaked—or dumped into a pot straight from a tin. Nowadays I prefer this mash made from fresh, sweet shelling peas—a twist on the British classic, which actually takes less work to make than its inspiration. It's wonderful spread in a thick layer on warm bread or as a dip for raw veg, like radishes, carrots, and wedges of fennel.

makes about 2 cups

2 cups fresh peas (from about 2 pounds pods)

1 ounce aged pecorino, finely grated

1½ teaspoons Maldon or another flaky sea salt

1 small spring garlic clove or ½ small garlic clove, smashed, peeled, and roughly chopped

12 medium mint leaves (preferably black mint)

3 tablespoons extra-virgin olive oil

Scant 2 tablespoons lemon juice, plus more for finishing

Combine the ingredients in a food processor and pulse to a coarse puree, about 45 seconds. Scrape the mixture into a bowl and roughly stir and smoosh a bit so it's a little creamy and a little chunky. Season to taste with more salt and lemon juice—you want it to taste sweet and bright but not acidic.

SNAP PEA SALAD

I admit that I'm hard on sugar snap peas. I get disappointed when they suck, of course, but I also get grumpy when they're anything less than perfect—unblemished, super sweet, and not a bit starchy. That's the curse of keeping high standards, I suppose: you're so rarely satisfied. When at last I do find perfect snap peas, I make this salad. I leave them raw—only the finest snap peas can be this delightful without a dunk in boiling water—and accentuate their flavor with little more than a lemony dressing and mint. If you'd like, you could add some creamy goat cheese in dollops or good old burrata alongside.

So long as you find the right snap peas, you'll have a smashing salad. But I find that putting your knife to them adds even more excitement, a little textural variation and attractiveness. Accordingly, run the tip of your knife along the spine of some of the larger pods, open them like a book to expose the peas, and gently pull to separate the two sides of the pod. Slice others diagonally in half or thirds. Keep small ones whole.

Combine the peas and mint in a large bowl. Pour in the dressing and toss gently but well. Season to taste with more salt and lemon, if you'd like. Add the arugula to the bowl and toss gently to coat the leaves in the dressing without bruising them. Arrange it all prettily on a platter and serve straightaway.

PREPPING SNAP PEAS

If you wish to remove the maximum string from your snap peas, try this: With one hand, hold a snap pea so the concave side is facing you and the stem end is facing down. With the other, use a small, sharp knife to cut just below the very tip of the pea and pull toward you, removing the string in the process. Rotate the pea so the stem end is facing up and the concave side is facing away from you. Now cut just below the tip of the pea and pull toward you, removing the string along the spine of the pea. This goes quite quickly once you get the hang of it, and you never have to worry about a stringy bit mucking up a good bite.

serves 4 as a side

1 pound sugar snap peas, trimmed and strings removed (see note)

A five-finger pinch of mint leaves (preferably black mint), roughly chopped at the last minute

¼ cup Simple Lemon Dressing (page 238)

Maldon or another flaky sea salt

Lemon juice

A large handful of delicate, peppery arugula

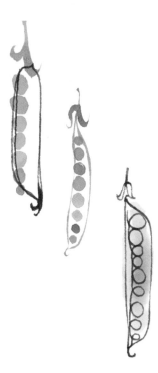

BRAISED PEAS AND LITTLE GEM LETTUCE

To me, this dish, also known as *petits pois à la française*, is a classic because the whole is so much greater than the sum of its parts. The dish isn't a vehicle for the peas or the braised lettuce to be the star; instead it's all about the magic they create together. The lettuce heads become silky and meaty, the sweet peas pop in your mouth, and all that springtime flavor infuses the broth. This dish would be delightful with duck confit, roast duck, or grilled lamb alongside, though if you're not in a meaty mood, stir in some cooked barley and you'll have a hearty meal.

Remove and reserve the floppy outer leaves from the lettuce, discarding any blemished ones. Halve the heads lengthwise. Rinse, drain, and thinly slice the reserved outer leaves.

Heat ¼ cup of the olive oil in a wide heavy pot over medium-high heat until it shimmers. Add the garlic and cook, occasionally flipping and stirring the cloves, until they're golden brown, 1 to 2 minutes. Use a slotted spoon to transfer the garlic to a small bowl.

Add the lettuce heads cut sides down to the pot (don't be alarmed if they spit and pop a bit) and cook until golden brown, 1 to 2 minutes. Turn them over, add ½ teaspoon or so of salt, and cook just until they've gone translucent at the stem and wilted at the tips, about 3 minutes more. It's OK if a few leaves fall off. Transfer the halved heads to a plate. Add the sliced lettuce, along with another ½ teaspoon or so of salt, to the pot and cook just until wilted and just about all the liquid in the pot has evaporated, about 2 minutes. Transfer to a medium bowl.

Give the pot a wipe, reduce the heat to medium-low, and add the remaining 2 tablespoons of oil and the butter. When the butter froths, add the onions and the cooked garlic along with 1 teaspoon of salt, have a stir, and cover the pot. Cook, stirring occasionally to make sure everything's happy, until the onions are soft and creamy but not

serves 6 as a side

3 heads Little Gem lettuce (about 1 pound), stems trimmed of brown but kept intact

¼ cup plus 2 tablespoons extra-virgin olive oil, plus a glug for finishing

6 medium spring garlic cloves or 3 medium garlic cloves, peeled and halved lengthwise

About 1 tablespoon Maldon or another flaky sea salt

1 tablespoon unsalted butter

1 pound young onions (see "Young Onions," page 49) or Spanish onions, halved lengthwise and cut crosswise into ¼-inch-thick slices

½ cup dry white wine, such as Sauvignon Blanc

2 cups shelled fresh peas (from about 2 pounds pods)

1½ cups Simple Chicken Stock (page 245)

A five-finger pinch of mint leaves (preferably black mint), roughly chopped at the last minute colored, about 20 minutes. Increase the heat to high, pour in the wine, and boil until it's nearly all evaporated, about 5 minutes.

Add the peas and return the cooked sliced lettuce to the pot, stir well, then return the lettuce head halves, cut sides up, to the pot along with the stock and 1 teaspoon of salt. Bring the stock to a boil, then reduce the heat to maintain a steady simmer, prodding the lettuce heads and peas a bit so they're nearly submerged. Cook just until the peas are soft but still pop in your mouth and the flavors marry, about 15 minutes, depending on the size of the peas.

Add the mint and a healthy glug of olive oil and have a stir. Add salt to taste. I like to let it cool a bit before I dig in.

RAMPS WITH FRIED EGGS

As simple a dish as I can imagine, this heap of sweet, garlicky ramps, bright from lemon and chile, is something I'd eat every day—if only those stubborn ramps didn't have such a short season. Yet that's part of their magic, isn't it? You can't always have them.

I like to eat the whole lot on toast. I like it with home fries. Sometimes I'll fry up a few strips of bacon first, until they're still a little bit floppy, then cook the ramps in the fat. The eggs make the dish all the more satisfying, though you can leave them out and serve the ramps as a side dish. Whether you use chicken or duck eggs, which are fattier and have a bit more character, make sure your oil is nice and hot so that when you crack in those eggs, the whites pop and spit and develop gorgeous crispy edges.

Halve any ramp bulbs thicker than a medium garlic clove. Cut the purple stems into 1-inch lengths and slice the leaves crosswise into thirds.

Combine the butter and oil in a 12-inch nonstick skillet and set it over medium heat. When the butter melts, froths, and gurgles, add the stems and bulbs, increase the heat to medium-high, and cook until the bulbs turn translucent, 2 to 3 minutes.

Add a generous pinch of salt to the pan and then sprinkle the leaves on top of the bulbs and stems. Stir briefly and shake the pan to dis-

serves 4 as a main

¾ pound ramps, trimmed and separated into white bulbs, purple stems, and green leaves (see note opposite)

5 tablespoons unsalted butter, cut into chunks

3 tablespoons extra-virgin olive oil

Maldon or another flaky sea salt

4 large duck or chicken eggs

2 dried pequín chiles, crumbled, or pinches of red pepper flakes

½ lemon

tribute the greens evenly and let it all sizzle away, stirring occasionally, until the bulbs have spots of golden brown, about 6 minutes more. Use a slotted spoon to transfer the ramps to a plate, leaving behind as much fat as you can.

With the pan still over medium-high heat, crack the eggs into the pan, trying your best to leave a little space between each one. Sprinkle the chiles and a generous pinch of salt over each egg. Cook until the whites have just set, about 1 minute. Spoon the ramp mixture here and there over the eggs but not over the yolks.

Cover the pan, turn off the heat, and let sit until the eggs are cooked to your liking, 1 to 2 minutes for nice runny yolks. Season with salt to taste and squeeze on just enough lemon juice to add brightness, not acidity. Eat straightaway.

Note: When they first appear in markets, ramp bulbs are so sweet and slender that you can add them all at once with the stems and leaves, though here I have you start the bulbs and stems a couple minutes early, in case they're a bit starchy, which can happen further into the season.

put a spring in your step

POT-ROASTED ARTICHOKES WITH WHITE WINE AND CAPERS

One of the reasons I go giddy about springtime is artichokes, particularly the small ones with tips closed tightly, like a flower at night. Some home cooks are reluctant to fill their totes with artichokes, as they'll need to be turned—the barbed leaves plucked off and the other inedible bits trimmed away. I quite like the process. It's meditative and satisfying once you get the hang of it. In this dish, the fleshy artichokes get browned and crispy tops and look like strange, beautiful roses. The acidity in the white wine cuts through the rich, dense veg and, along with the salty pops from the capers, highlights the artichokes' unique herbaceousness.

Heat the oil in a heavy pot (wide enough to hold the artichokes with room to spare) over medium-high heat until it just begins to smoke. Stand the artichokes cut sides down in the oil, wait a minute, then reduce the heat to medium-low, sprinkle in the garlic and salt, and cook, without stirring, just until the garlic turns golden and smells toasty, about 3 minutes.

Slowly pour in the wine, cover the pot, and cook, without stirring, at a vigorous simmer until you can insert a sharp knife into the thick artichoke bottoms with barely any resistance, about 25 minutes. Five minutes or so before they're fully tender, remove the lid and scatter on the capers.

Raise the heat to medium-high, and bring the liquid to a boil. Cook until all the wine has evaporated (the bubbling sound will become a sizzle), about 3 minutes. Add the mint and parsley and keep cooking the artichokes in the oil (it's OK if a few of them tip over), until the cut sides of the artichokes are deep golden brown, 3 to 5 minutes. Lower the heat if necessary to prevent the artichokes from getting too dark.

Arrange the artichokes prettily on a plate, and scoop the capers, oil, and slightly crispy herbs over top. Serve straightaway or at room temperature.

serves 4 to 6 as a side

¼ cup extra-virgin olive oil

3½ pounds baby artichokes (about 18), turned (see "Turning Artichokes," page 32)

2 medium garlic cloves, thinly sliced

1½ teaspoons Maldon or another flaky sea salt

1½ cups dry white wine, such as Sauvignon Blanc

1 heaping tablespoon drained capers

A five-finger pinch of mint leaves (preferably black mint), torn at the last minute

A pinch of delicate flat-leaf parsley sprigs

TURNING ARTICHOKES

I suppose some people might find it a bother, but I quite like turning artichokes. It's like an advanced version of shelling peas—similarly meditative and even a bit fun. Choosing artichokes whose leaves don't move much when you pinch the tops will make your life a bit easier, because typically they have smaller chokes or sometimes none at all.

Fill a big bowl with water and squeeze in the juice of a lemon. Working with one artichoke at a time, pluck off and discard the green leaves until only the soft yellowish leaves are left. Cut off about ½ inch of the stem. Use a peeler or small knife to trim away the tough green stuff at the base of the artichoke. Take a peek at the cut end of the stem. You'll see a pale green circle surrounded by a darker border. Peel the stem, getting as close as you can to the pale green center. Drop the artichoke into the lemony water (to prevent discoloration). Repeat with the remaining artichokes.

Cut about 1 inch from the tip of each artichoke, then use a small spoon to scoop out and discard the feathery choke. Gently squeeze each artichoke over the bowl as you go, and set them cut sides down on paper towels to drain for about 5 minutes.

BOILED ASPARAGUS WITH RAMP BÉARNAISE SAUCE

Sometimes what seems like the least exciting way to cook a vegetable is the most lovely. I adore roasted and grilled asparagus, with those tempting golden-brown spots. Still, my favorite way to eat asparagus is boiled. That's when it feels the most elegant in the mouth, fat and juicy and clean when you bite it.

The stalks require little more than a drizzle of nice olive oil and perhaps a spritz of lemon, but an even more thrilling accompaniment is a rich, bright béarnaise served alongside. It's the sexiest thing, a béarnaise. I must've made this tart, rich French sauce, a sort of hot mayonnaise made with butter instead of oil, a thousand times when I worked under Rowley Leigh at the London restaurant Kensington Place. I don't think I ever got tired of dipping vegetables in it or drizzling it over grilled fish or steak. In early spring, when ramps join bunches of asparagus at farmers' markets, I swap the typical shallots for ramp bulbs and finish the sauce with ramp leaves instead of the more classic tarragon.

You can make béarnaise a few hours in advance, so long as you keep it somewhere warm. If you keep it somewhere too hot or chilly, it could split. To fix split béarnaise, add 1 teaspoon of warm water to a bowl, then add the béarnaise bit by bit, starting with a few drops and upping the amount as you go, whisking furiously with each addition.

make the béarnaise

Combine the vinegar and the ramp bulbs and stems in a small saucepan. Bring the liquid to a gentle simmer over medium-low heat and cook, swirling occasionally, until the vinegar has fully evaporated, 5 to 8 minutes. Let the mixture cool slightly.

Fill a small pot with an inch or so of water and bring the water to a boil. Grab a heatproof mixing bowl that will fit in the pot without touching the water. Combine the ramp mixture, egg yolks, and the tablespoon of hot water in the bowl and whisk well. Set the bowl in

serves 4 as a side

FOR THE BÉARNAISE

½ cup Champagne vinegar or white wine vinegar

Scant ½ pound ramps, trimmed, green leaves separated, and everything thinly sliced (about ½ cup bulbs and stems and 1 cup leaves)

2 large egg yolks

1 tablespoon hot water, plus more if necessary

1 cup Clarified Butter (page 37), warm

1 teaspoon Maldon or another flaky sea salt, or more to taste

FOR THE ASPARAGUS

Kosher salt

1 pound asparagus (spears as thick as an index finger), woody bottoms snapped off

the pot and whisk constantly, scraping the sides of the bowl as you do and lifting the bowl from the pot every 15 seconds or so. You want to cook the yolks as gently as possible. Keep at it just until the mixture has thickened to the texture of loose mayonnaise, about 2 minutes.

Remove the bowl from the pot and wrap a damp kitchen towel around the base of the bowl to steady it. Drizzle in the clarified butter in a very slow, steady stream, whisking constantly. (If after you've added half the butter, the mixture looks really thick and shiny, whisk in another tablespoon of hot water before you add the rest of the butter.) Stir in the salt and ramp leaves, taste, and season with salt to taste.

Set the béarnaise aside in a warm place.

make the asparagus
Bring a medium pot of water to a boil over high heat and season it generously with salt until it's a little less salty than the sea.

Add the asparagus and cook just until the asparagus is cooked through but still snappy and juicy (the spears should give slightly when you give them a gentle squeeze), 2 to 3 minutes. Use tongs or a spider to gently remove the asparagus. Drain it well, pat it dry, and arrange it on a platter. Serve the béarnaise in a bowl alongside for dipping or drizzle it prettily over the top.

CLARIFIED BUTTER

When I plan to make béarnaise, hollandaise, and many other emulsified French sauces, my first step is to clarify butter, or melt the butter and cook it slowly so the milk solids rise to the surface to be skimmed off, leaving behind only the glass-clear yellow fat. Using this instead of regular melted butter is essential for achieving a sauce of the proper texture and also one that won't readily split on you. Even if you're not planning to make my ramp béarnaise (page 35), you should still give clarifying butter a go. For one, it's good fun to have an excuse to melt a big old hunk of butter, taking plenty of sniffs as it bubbles away. Clarified butter also makes a great cooking fat, since it won't burn at high temperatures like regular butter will.

makes about 2¼ cups

1½ pounds (6 sticks) unsalted butter,
cut into about 1½-inch pieces

Put the butter in a medium saucepan and set it over medium-low heat. Let it melt completely, without stirring, until it begins to bubble, then have a gentle stir. Let the butter bubble steadily, without stirring, lowering the heat if you spot any browning around the edges. Some of the whitish milk solids will rise to the surface, some will cook off, and some will settle at the bottom of the pan. Cook until the yellow liquid is nearly transparent (you'll want to push the white solids on the surface aside to have a good look at the liquid), 10 to 12 minutes.

Use a spoon to gently skim the white stuff from the surface. You should be left with transparent golden fat with some opaque milk solids below. Slowly pour the yellow liquid butter into a container, leaving any remaining milk solids behind in the pan.

The clarified butter keeps in an airtight container for up to a month in the refrigerator.

SPRING EGG DROP SOUP

I hate muddling through a long winter only to suffer those odd early spring months when the weather is finally warming up, but the markets don't seem to have noticed. Spring produce takes a while to shake off the cold. So when it does, an excitable cook like me tends to go overboard. I pop to the market to grab a bunch of asparagus and return weighed down by bags and bags of spring goodies. I want to use them all without cooking a dozen different dishes. So I make a nice soup, one flaunting a last-minute drizzle of eggs beaten with a little Parmesan so they set in silky, fatty strands. A variety of veg is fantastic here, but feel free to use just asparagus or just peas, if that's what you've got or what you like.

Heat the oil in a wide heavy pot over medium heat until it shimmers. Add the carrots first, then the onion, garlic, and 2 teaspoons of the salt. Cover and cook, stirring only after 5 minutes have passed and occasionally thereafter, until the onions are soft and creamy but not colored, about 25 minutes.

Uncover, add all but 1 tablespoon of the chicken stock, increase the heat to high, and bring the stock to a vigorous simmer. Add the asparagus and both kinds of peas and cook just until they're tender with a slight crunch, about 3 minutes.

Meanwhile, beat the eggs with the Parmesan, a pinch of salt, and the remaining tablespoon of stock.

When the green vegetables are ready, reduce the heat to low, stir in the herbs, then drizzle the egg mixture here and there over the soup. Have one very gentle stir, wait a minute or two until the egg sets, then take the pot off the heat. Season to taste with salt (be judicious, or else you will obscure the flavor of the vegetables), then squeeze in just enough lemon to add brightness, not acidity. Let the soup cool slightly before you dig in.

serves 4

¼ cup extra-virgin olive oil

½ pound young carrots, topped, tailed, peeled, and cut into ½-inch irregularly shaped pieces

2 cups chopped (½-inch pieces) bulbous spring onions

3 slim or 1 bulbous spring garlic head(s), roots and tops trimmed, tough layers removed, thinly sliced

2 teaspoons plus a pinch Maldon or another flaky sea salt

4 cups Simple Chicken Stock (page 245)

½ pound asparagus, woody bottoms snapped off, cut on the diagonal into ½-inch pieces

¼ pound sugar snap peas, trimmed, strings removed, and cut on the diagonal into ¼-inch pieces

⅔ cup shelled fresh peas (from about ⅔ pound pods)

2 large eggs

2 tablespoons finely grated Parmesan cheese

A five-finger pinch of mint leaves (preferably black mint), roughly chopped at the last minute

A five-finger pinch of basil leaves, roughly chopped at the last minute

½ lemon

WATERCRESS SOUP
WITH SPRING GARLIC

The watercress I dream about comes from Dave Harris at Max Creek Hatchery, in Delaware County, New York. "Hatchery?" you might wonder. Yes, Dave deals mainly in trout, fresh and smoked, but he also sells perfectly peppery, bitter watercress that grows wild by the water. He keeps sheep, too, that like to chomp on it while they're grazing. Sheep eat everything, those little buggers. This soup features the sophisticated flavor of watercress balanced by the sweetness of slowly cooked onion and spring garlic. The soup's silky body comes from potatoes, rinsed to wash away some of their starch, and, if I'm being honest, plenty of tasty fat. Fortunately, watercress is one of those vegetables whose strong flavor lets you know you're eating something good for you. I like to think that's all that matters. Add a spoonful of smoked trout roe for a special treat.

The soup will go from garden green to drab olive if you don't serve it straightaway. If you'd like to make the soup the night before but retain its bright green color, make an ice-water bath in a bowl large enough to hold another bowl and set the second large bowl in the bath. Once the soup is done, pour it in the bowl and stir until it's cold. Transfer it to an airtight container and keep it in the fridge for up to a day.

Trim away the roots and cut off and discard the dark green tops of the spring garlic. Peel off the outermost layer from the stalks and bulbs. If your knife slides easily through the stalk about 4 inches up from the bulb, thinly slice it and set aside. If not, save it to use as an aromatic in stock or sauce. Halve the bulbs lengthwise and if necessary remove any tough layers. Thinly slice the bulb, discarding anything you come across with which your knife struggles.

Melt the butter in a medium pot over medium-low heat, then add the garlic, onion, and 1 tablespoon of the salt and have a stir. Cover the pot and cook, stirring occasionally and reducing the heat if the onion threatens to color, until the onion is very soft, creamy, and sweet, about 30 minutes.

serves 4 to 6

2 spring garlic heads, with stalks attached if possible (see "Spring Garlic," opposite)

¼ pound (1 stick) plus 2 tablespoons unsalted butter

1 large Spanish onion (about 1 pound), halved lengthwise and thinly sliced

2½ tablespoons plus a pinch Maldon or another flaky sea salt

1 pound russet (baking) potatoes, peeled, cut into ½-inch pieces, rinsed, and drained well

2 cups whole milk

1 pound mature watercress (not baby), bottom inch of stems trimmed, thick stems thinly sliced, the rest left whole

A small handful of delicate chervil sprigs, optional

½ cup plus 1 teaspoon extra-virgin olive oil

½ cup crème fraîche

½ teaspoon black peppercorns, toasted in a small pan until aromatic, then coarsely crushed

Add the potatoes, milk, the remaining 1½ tablespoons of salt, and 2 cups of water. Cover the pot, increase the heat to medium, and bring the liquid to a vigorous simmer. Uncover, lower the heat if necessary to maintain a gentle simmer, and cook until the potatoes are fully tender, about 15 minutes.

Add the watercress and chervil (if you're using it), let it wilt slightly, and gently stir to submerge the greens in the liquid. Bring the mixture back to a simmer, pour in ½ cup of the oil, then remove the pot from the heat.

Pour the soup into a large mixing bowl. Working in batches, blend the soup (be careful when blending hot liquids) until very smooth, adding each batch back to the pot. (Whenever I make this at one of my restaurants, I use a high-power blender, such as a Vita-Prep, to get the soup especially smooth and fully bright green rather than green-flecked.)

Keep the soup warm in the pot and season to taste with salt. Combine the crème fraîche and crushed peppercorns in a small bowl with the remaining 1 teaspoon of olive oil and a pinch of salt and stir well.

Divide the soup among bowls, top with the crème fraîche mixture, and serve straightaway.

SPRING GARLIC

At farmers' markets, you see spring garlic in different sizes. For this recipe, try to find bulbous heads that are close in size to a head of standard garlic. Sometimes, especially in early spring, the spring garlic on offer might have slim heads, about the size of green onion bottoms. These are just fine, though you'll want to use 6 or so, including the tender parts of the stalks. Even on the larger bulbs of spring garlic, there's a chance that the bottom four or so inches of stalk will also be tender enough to use in this recipe.

ASPARAGUS QUICHES WITH MINT

I'm afraid that quiche has gone out of fashion, hasn't it? I think I know why. When I was growing up, I ate some truly horrible ones, both home-cooked and store-bought, packed with what seemed like a refrigerator's worth of odds and ends suspended in overcooked egg. The only fun I'd have eating them was squidging the filling through my teeth. But as with most foods we think we don't like, a truly excellent specimen can change our minds in a bite. My hope is that this quiche does just that with a delicate, flaky crust and an eggy filling that's fluffy enough to banish those bad memories forever.

You *could* eat quiche piping hot from the oven, of course, but I prefer it once it's cooled a bit or at room temperature. Fresh from the oven, quiche tastes mostly of crust. Only when it cools does it all balance out, the crust stepping back a few paces and the egginess and filling marching forward to say hello.

Quiche makes a great vehicle for whatever vegetables are in season and a fun way to impress when you have a crowd over for lunch. Little quiches are really cute, but feel free to make one larger quiche, if you fancy. An 11-inch tart pan will do it, though you will wind up with some extra dough.

make the dough

Combine the flour, sugar, kosher salt, and baking powder in a food processor and pulse several times to mix them well. Add the butter and pulse until the mixture has the texture of fine breadcrumbs. A few pebble-size pieces of butter here and there is just fine.

Transfer the mixture to a bowl, pour in the crème fraîche and water, and use your fingertips to toss and gently smoosh the mixture just until it comes together as a dry, slightly crumbly dough. Don't over-work it and don't let it warm up too much. Cover the bowl and keep it in the fridge for 15 to 30 minutes.

Line your work surface and a baking sheet with parchment paper. Turn the dough onto the work surface and roll it out to an even

makes twelve 3-inch quiches

SPECIAL EQUIPMENT

Twelve 3-inch-wide, 1-inch-deep ring molds or tartlet pans

FOR THE DOUGH

3¼ cups all-purpose flour

1 teaspoon sugar

½ teaspoon kosher salt

¼ teaspoon baking powder

½ pound (2 sticks) unsalted butter, well chilled and cut into ½-inch pieces

¼ cup crème fraîche

¼ cup very cold water

FOR THE FILLING

Kosher salt

1 pound asparagus (spears as thick as an index finger), woody bottoms snapped off, stalks cut into ¼-inch pieces, tips left whole (about 2¾ cups total)

3 tablespoons unsalted butter, cut into several chunks

1 cup finely diced Spanish onion (about 1 small)

¼-inch thickness, dusting the dough with flour if the rolling pin sticks to it. Trace an inverted bowl with the tip of your knife to cut out twelve 4½-inch rounds. Work swiftly to line each ring mold with a dough round, pressing the sides and bottoms gently. Put them on the baking sheet, cover them with plastic wrap, and refrigerate for at least 4 hours or overnight.

bake the shells

Position a rack in the center of the oven and preheat to 325°F.

Cut parchment paper into twelve 5-inch squares. Crumple each square into a ball, wet the ball under running water, squeeze out all the water, and flatten them out again. (This makes them more malleable.) Just before you're ready to bake the shells (not sooner), take them from the fridge. (They must be nice and cold when you pop them in the oven, or else your quiches will be greasy.) Use one square of parchment paper to line each shell and fill each one almost to the brim with dried beans or raw rice. (You can save the rice or beans to use the next time you bake.) Put the shells back in the fridge for about 15 minutes.

Bake, rotating the baking sheet once, just until the dough is no longer raw but not yet colored at all, 20 to 25 minutes. Remove the beans or rice and parchment squares. Gently prick the bottom and sides of the dough with a fork, which will prevent it from puffing up as it bakes. Return to the oven and bake until the shells are evenly light golden brown and the edges have pulled away from the sides of the pans, 25 to 30 minutes. Let the shells cool completely before you fill them. Leave the oven on.

make the filling and assemble the quiche

Bring a medium pot of water to a boil and salt it generously until it's slightly less salty than the sea. Cook the asparagus stalks in the water just until they've lost their raw crunch, 1 to 1½ minutes, using

1 small bulb spring garlic, tough outer layer removed, bulb thinly sliced and then roughly chopped, or 1 tablespoon thinly sliced regular garlic

¼ teaspoon Maldon or another flaky sea salt

2 large eggs plus 2 large egg yolks

¾ cup heavy cream

¾ cup whole milk

8 mint leaves (preferably black mint), thinly sliced at the last minute

45

a spider to transfer them to a colander to drain. Do the same with the tips, keeping them separate from the stalks.

Melt the butter in a medium skillet over medium-low heat until frothy. Add the onion, garlic, and Maldon salt and cook, stirring now and again, until the onion is soft and just barely browned at the edges, about 12 minutes. Remove the pan from the heat.

Combine the whole eggs and egg yolks in a large bowl and whisk briefly. Combine the cream and milk in a small pot, set it over medium-high heat, and cook just until it reaches a strong simmer. Immediately remove it from the heat, then very gradually pour it into the bowl with the eggs, whisking as you pour. Stir in 2 teaspoons of kosher salt. Let the egg mixture, onion mixture, and asparagus come to room temperature.

Divide the onion mixture among the shells, spreading slightly to form a layer. Spoon in the asparagus stalks (about 2 generous tablespoons per shell). Whisk the egg mixture, then ladle in enough of it to come up to about ¼ inch from the rim. Add the asparagus tips (two or three per quiche) and the mint. Pull the oven rack forward and carefully transfer the tray to the rack, then top off each quiche with a little more egg mixture. (This way the quiches won't spill as you transport them to the oven.)

Bake the quiches, rotating the baking sheet once, just until the egg mixture has set, 20 to 25 minutes. It should no longer be liquidy, but should still be soft and moist to the touch.

Remove the molds (or, if using tartlet pans, let the quiches cool slightly before carefully removing the quiches) and let the quiches cool slightly or to room temperature before you dig in.

ROASTED YOUNG ONIONS WITH SAGE PESTO

My knees go a bit wobbly when I pull these onions out of the oven, because I know they've given up every last bit of bite and become wonderfully creamy. They taste so sweet, you'll have a hard time convincing people that all you did was roast them with salt and olive oil. No embellishment is necessary, but salty, woodsy sage pesto sure makes a nice one.

Position a rack in the center of the oven and preheat to 350°F.

Cut off the onion greens, leaving just ½ inch or so above the bulb. Peel off the thin, leathery outer layer of each onion and trim off the spidery roots, but make sure to leave the little nub intact (that is, the tough flat part the roots protrude from). This will keep the onions from falling apart as they cook. Halve each onion lengthwise and sprinkle the cut sides with a few healthy pinches of salt.

Find an ovenproof skillet or heavy enameled baking dish wide enough to hold the onion halves in a single layer with a little room to spare. Add 3 tablespoons of the oil to the pan and set it over high heat until the oil just begins to smoke. Lower the heat to medium and carefully add the onions cut sides down and cook, using tongs to peek under the onions occasionally, until you see spots of golden brown, 5 to 8 minutes.

Pop the pan in the oven and cook until the cut sides are an even deeper golden brown but have no black spots, 20 to 25 minutes. Carefully turn the onions over with tongs and raise the oven temperature to 425°F. Continue cooking until the onions are very soft but not falling apart, 10 to 15 minutes more.

Meanwhile, put the sage in a small food processor with the garlic, pine nuts, Parmesan, and 1 teaspoon of salt and pulse several times. Add the remaining ½ cup of oil to the mixture and process full-on,

serves 4 to 6 as a side

6 young onions (the size of tennis balls), yellow, red, or a combination (see "Young Onions," opposite)

Maldon or another flaky sea salt

½ cup plus 3 tablespoons extra-virgin olive oil

A big handful of sage leaves

1 small garlic clove, roughly chopped

3 tablespoons pine nuts

1 ounce Parmesan cheese, finely grated

stopping to scrape down the sides and stir gently if necessary, until the mixture is well combined but still chunky.

Arrange the onions prettily on a plate. Spoon some pesto, as much as you like, here and there on top of the onions. (Reserve the remaining pesto for another day.) Eat straightaway.

YOUNG ONIONS

At farmers' markets in the spring, you'll spot piles of onions with their greens attached. The onion bulbs will either be slim, like those of scallions, or bulbous. I think of the former as spring onions. I think of the latter, which are what you want for this recipe, as young onions, because their bulbs are big enough to become sweet and creamy in the oven but haven't yet been left to cure and develop the papery skins of mature onions. I'm reluctant to say that you can substitute mature red onions, which have a sharper bite, because the result won't be quite as sweet and delicious. Reluctant, but not opposed.

the
humble potato

BOILED POTATOES WITH BUTTER AND MINT

I never get bored with potatoes. They're one of those quietly wonderful vegetables. The potato isn't flashy. It doesn't advertise with bright colors like tomatoes or carrots. It's not a fleeting beauty like ramps. It doesn't have the big, sweet flavor of corn or peas. The potato, rather, is comforting and always there for you—even throughout the long winters in the Northeast. The potato is like a good mate you've known forever.

I discovered my affection for the potato in primary school. Me and my little friends would storm the cafeteria at lunch. Most of the food was rubbish, except the buttery boiled potatoes, which I'd eat by the pile. This is my grown-up version. It's barely more complicated—the mint adds brightness and the lemon cuts through the starch and fat—but a lot more moreish. For you Yanks, moreish just means that each bite makes you want to eat more of it.

Put the potatoes and the salt in a medium straight-sided pan or small, shallow pot, add enough water to cover the potatoes by ½ inch or so, and set the pot over high heat. Bring the water to a boil, reduce the heat to maintain a vigorous simmer, and cook until fully tender and creamy inside, about 20 minutes. Reserving ¼ cup of the cooking liquid, drain the potatoes (gently so they don't break) and return them to the pot.

Add the butter, garlic, and reserved cooking liquid to the pot and set it over medium-high heat. Let the butter melt and the liquid bubble until the liquid looks milky, 1 to 2 minutes. Cook at a vigorous simmer, tilting the pan and swirling the liquid occasionally, until the liquid reduces to a slightly viscous glaze, about 5 minutes.

Add the mint, stir gently but well, and take the pot off the heat. Squeeze on just enough lemon juice to add brightness, not acidity, and add pepper and more salt to taste. Serve straightaway.

serves 4 as a side

1 pound small potatoes, such as fingerlings, all about the same size

1 tablespoon Maldon or another flaky sea salt

4 tablespoons (½ stick) unsalted butter, cut into several pieces

1 small garlic clove, finely grated on a rasp-style grater

A five-finger pinch of mint leaves (preferably black mint), roughly torn at the last minute

½ lemon

Coarsely ground black pepper

the humble potato **53**

simple things
potatoes

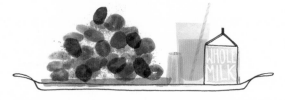

You'll find many recipes for potatoes in this book. But my love for the lowly potato began at my school cafeteria with this simple preparation: boiled and buttered. Making them at home requires no recipe, just a bit of care and attention.

First, you must find potatoes with some character. Back in England, I'd go mad for the Jersey Royal. This is a springtime potato grown in the soil of Jersey, the French-speaking island in the English Channel. Farmers there use seaweed as fertilizer, just one of the reasons that these are extra special potatoes: earthy, sweet, and creamy. Here in the States, any new potatoes—those dug before they've reached maturity and all the sugars have turned to starch—hit the spot. They're so good that your only job as a cook is not to muck them up.

So long as you give the potatoes a good rinse and gentle rub with your fingers, you can leave the thin skins on. If some of the potatoes are larger than others, cut them into similarly sized pieces, so they'll all be done at the same time. Pop them into a pot, add enough water to cover them by an inch or so, and add plenty of salt, because starchy things like potatoes don't absorb salt easily. You should add enough salt so that when it dissolves the water will taste a little less salty than the sea does.

Bring the water to a boil, then reduce the heat to maintain a steady simmer—the larger the potatoes, the more gentle the simmer should be to ensure even cooking—and cook until they're tender and creamy. To tell when they're done, here's a trick I learned: stick a small sharp knife into one of the potatoes, then lift the knife—if the potato comes up with the knife then slides right off by itself, the potatoes are done. Just don't get poke happy or the potatoes will get waterlogged. Drain the potatoes carefully in a colander, then let them sit for a few minutes so some water escapes as steam. While they're still hot, put them in a bowl and toss them with plenty of butter, cut into pieces, until it melts. Top with coarsely ground black pepper and a nice sprinkling of salt, if you'd like.

SALT-CRUSTED POTATOES WITH HERBED VINEGAR

Here's a nice, unusual way to cook my old pal the potato. For the typical boiled potatoes, I'd simmer them gently in salty water. For this preparation, the bubbles are furious. In fact, you're meant to boil the water not just until the potatoes are cooked but until it evaporates altogether. (While I do it, I like to think of a salt lake drying out to become a salt flat.) The salt left behind coats each potato to form a toasty crust that reminds me of a perfect baked potato with an especially salty jacket. Then all you do is spoon on a mixture of vinegar and fresh herbs. Just don't serve the potatoes in a bowl or stir them, or you'll lose the crust and the whole dish will get too salty.

Put the potatoes in a medium pot where they'll fit snugly in one layer and add enough cold water to just barely cover them. Add the salt and bring the water to a boil over high heat. Boil until the potatoes are tender and the water has completely evaporated, giving the pan an occasional shake once the water's almost all gone, 30 to 40 minutes. Keep cooking, and shaking, until the potatoes are coated with a layer of salt and the bottom of the pot has begun to brown (don't fret; it'll scrub off easily later), about 3 minutes more. Take the pot off the heat and let the potatoes cool slightly.

If any potatoes have a very thick layer of salt, gently rub them with a kitchen towel to knock a bit off. Halve the potatoes the long way and arrange them cut sides up on a large platter or plate. Whisk together the oil and vinegar in a small bowl until the mixture looks creamy. Toss the herbs together, coarsely chop them, and stir them into the vinegar mixture. Spoon the mixture over the potatoes, sprinkle on as much pepper as you'd like, and serve straightaway.

serves 4 to 6 as a side

2 pounds golf-ball-size Yukon Gold potatoes

3 tablespoons Jacobsen, Maldon, or another flaky sea salt

¼ cup extra-virgin olive oil

2 tablespoons red wine vinegar or sherry vinegar

A five-finger pinch of delicate flat-leaf parsley sprigs

6 or so large basil leaves

10 or so large mint leaves (preferably black mint)

Coarsely ground black pepper

HASSELBACK POTATOES WITH LARDO AND ROSEMARY

Rumor has it that these potatoes were invented at a restaurant in Stockholm called Hasselbacken. Whoever did come up with them is clever, indeed. The technique involves making parallel slits the length of the potato, cutting into but not completely through each spud and then roasting them, so they expand like an accordion and get extra crispy as they cook. The result is potatoes you want to eat with your hands.

When I make this dish, I like to tuck a sliver of lardo, Italian cured fatback, in some of those slits. As the potatoes cook, the lardo melts, basting the potatoes and going all crispy itself. Tucking in the lardo can be fiddly and take a while. (You might call it a bit of a *hassle*, if you don't mind bad puns.) Keep at it. Remember that lardo cooperates better when it's well chilled and that these are special-occasion potatoes that are worth the effort. But if you get really grumpy, stick to two or three pieces of lardo per potato rather than four or five.

Position a rack in the center of the oven and preheat to 400°F.

Working with one potato at a time, cut through the potato crosswise every ¼ to ⅛ inch as though you were cutting the potato into slices but stopping about ¼ inch before you reach the bottom. (I like to insert a thin skewer or cake tester lengthwise through the potato and stop cutting when I hit the skewer.) Repeat with the remaining potatoes. Rinse the potatoes well under water, carefully pulling open the slits to expose the flesh to the water, then drain well.

Cut the lardo slices crosswise into pieces about as long as the width of each potato. Tuck the pieces of lardo inside some of the slits (2 to 5 pieces per potato, depending on your mood), being careful not to break the potatoes. It's nice if a portion of each piece of lardo is sticking out. You might want to keep half the lardo in the fridge as you work, so it stays firm and is therefore easier to work with.

serves 4 to 6 as a side

2 pounds small creamer or other nonwaxy potatoes (about 16, each about the size and shape of an egg)

2 ounces thinly sliced lardo, well chilled

¼ cup extra-virgin olive oil

Maldon or another flaky sea salt

3 rosemary sprigs

Arrange the potatoes lardo side up in a heavy enameled baking dish large enough to fit them with a little space between each one. Drizzle on the oil, making sure each potato gets some, and sprinkle a healthy pinch of salt over each one. Bake the potatoes, rotating the dish occasionally, until the visible lardo turns golden brown and crisp and the slits begin to open up a bit, about 45 minutes.

Carefully tip the dish so the fat pools, then use a spoon to baste each potato. Keep cooking, basting once more, until the potato flesh is creamy, about 30 minutes more.

Baste once more, then flip the potatoes and cook until the bottoms look good and crispy, about 15 minutes.

Add the rosemary to the baking dish, resting some of the potatoes on and others near the sprigs so they pick up some of the rosemary's flavor, and cook for another 5 minutes or so. Baste once more, season with salt to taste, then transfer the potatoes to a plate, drizzling a little of the flavorful fat over top, if you wish. Serve straightaway.

PATATAS BRAVAS

There are two main versions of *patatas bravas*, the common Spanish tapas dish that features crispy fried potatoes: one that's drizzled with aioli and another that's topped with sweet, smoky tomato sauce. I prefer the second—to me, the first is just chips and mayonnaise, not that there's anything wrong with chips with mayonnaise—especially when the potatoes are tossed in the sauce and eaten straightaway, before they lose their crunch. They make an impressive side dish all by themselves, though fried eggs on top turn them into a proper meal for four.

make the sauce

Peel the skin from the bell peppers using a vegetable peeler and a gentle sawing motion. Cut the peppers into 1-inch pieces. Heat ¼ cup of the oil in a wide, heavy medium pot over high heat until it smokes lightly. Add the onion, chiles, garlic, and salt. Have a stir and cook, stirring occasionally, until the onions wilt a bit, about 3 minutes. Add the bell peppers and paprika, but don't stir until the onions begin to brown, about 3 minutes more. Now stir and cook, stirring and scraping the bottom often, until the onions and peppers are tender, about 10 minutes. Lower the heat to medium and keep stirring and scraping until everything is very soft and sweet, 12 to 15 minutes more.

Meanwhile, core and quarter the tomatoes, put them in a large mixing bowl, and gently squeeze to release the juice and seeds. Transfer the tomatoes to a second large bowl, leaving the liquid and seeds behind, shaking the tomatoes over the first bowl so any liquid caught in the crevices spills out. Set a strainer over the bowl with the tomatoes and pour the liquid through the strainer, smooshing to make sure you extract as much liquid as you can and discarding the solids.

Add the tomatoes and their liquid to the pot, stir, and cook at a steady simmer, stirring now and then, until most of the visible liquid has evaporated, 45 minutes to 1 hour. Stir in the marjoram. Keep cooking, stirring and scraping the pot often, until the sauce starts to stick to

serves 6 to 8 as a side

SPECIAL EQUIPMENT

An electric deep-fryer (preferable) or a large, heavy pot (such as a Dutch oven) and a deep-fry thermometer, and a spider

FOR THE SAUCE

1½ pounds red bell peppers (about 3 medium), halved lengthwise, seeded, and deribbed

¼ cup extra-virgin olive oil, plus a good drizzle for finishing

1 large Spanish onion (about 1¼ pounds), halved and cut into ¼-inch-thick slices

Scant ¼ pound moderately spicy fresh red chiles (such as Dutch or Fresno), halved lengthwise, stemmed, and roughly chopped (including seeds)

4 medium garlic cloves, thinly sliced

2 teaspoons Maldon or another flaky sea salt

1 teaspoon sweet smoked Spanish paprika (pimentón dulce)

3 pounds tomatoes, peeled (see page 16)

the bottom of the pot and the mixture is very thick, a bit like jam, about 10 minutes more. Take the pot off the heat.

fry the potatoes

Put the potatoes in a medium pot, pour in enough water to cover, and add enough kosher salt to make the water taste good and salty. Bring the water to a boil over high heat. Lower the heat to maintain a simmer and cook until the potatoes are just tender, about 5 minutes. Drain the potatoes well in a colander, then gently shake and toss them in the colander just until the potatoes get a bit fluffy looking on the outsides. (The rough sides will get especially crispy when the potatoes are fried.) Let them sit uncovered until they've cooled to room temperature.

Meanwhile, pour at least 3 inches of fat or oil into an electric deep-fryer (or into a Dutch oven with a deep-fry thermometer clipped to the side) and heat to 300°F. Working in batches (to avoid crowding), fry the potatoes until they develop a creamy texture (they shouldn't be browned at all), about 5 minutes. As they cook, shake the fry basket or gently stir occasionally to prevent them from sticking together. Use a spider to transfer the potatoes to a bowl and give them a gentle toss so they have another chance to go fluffy.

Bring the fat or oil temperature to 350°F. Line a bowl or tray with paper towels. Fry the potatoes again in batches, stirring occasionally, until they're very crispy and deep golden brown on the outsides, about 15 minutes. Transfer them to the towels to drain and immediately add a light sprinkle of Maldon salt.

Just before the potatoes are done, bring the sauce to a sizzle.

The key to the next step is doing it seconds before you serve the dish, so the potatoes stay a bit crispy: add the fried potatoes to the sauce, stir briefly but well, and transfer the sauced potatoes to a plate. Add a good drizzle of olive oil and more salt if you fancy. Serve straightaway.

A small handful of marjoram leaves, roughly chopped at the last minute

FOR THE POTATOES

3 pounds Yukon Gold or russet potatoes, peeled, cut into irregular 1-inch pieces, and rinsed well

Kosher salt

Rendered duck fat, pork fat, or peanut oil for deep-frying

Maldon or another flaky sea salt

POTATO SOUP WITH GARLIC AND PARSLEY

If I could get away with opening a restaurant that served only boiled potatoes with butter and black pepper, I just might. Of course, customers expect a bit more from a chef than boiled potatoes, however delicious they may be. This soup is my attempt at a middle ground between plain boiled and don't-try-this-at-home knotty—it's barely more complicated than its inspiration, but a bit more elegant. The magic of starch gives the soup a luxurious velvety texture, and the toasty garlic and parsley stirred in last minute give each slurp extra complexity.

make the soup

Heat the oil in a large pot over high heat until it smokes lightly. Add the butter, onion, garlic, and salt and stir. Cover the pot and reduce the heat to medium-low. Cook, stirring now and again, until the onions are very soft and creamy but not colored at all, about 25 minutes. If you spot any browning, reduce the heat.

Add the potatoes and stock to the pot. Cover the pot, raise the heat to high, and bring to a boil. Uncover the pot and lower the heat to maintain a steady simmer. Simmer until the potatoes are very tender, about 25 minutes.

Pour the soup into a large mixing bowl. Working in batches, blend the soup (be careful when blending hot liquids) until very smooth and silky, adding each batch back to the pot. Keep it warm over very low heat while you prepare the garnish. (The soup keeps covered in the fridge for a day or two. When you're ready to serve it, reheat it gently until it's good and hot.)

finish the soup

Just before you serve the soup, heat the olive oil in a medium skillet over high heat until it smokes lightly. Add the garlic and cook, shak-

serves 6 to 8

FOR THE SOUP

¼ cup extra-virgin olive oil

2 tablespoons unsalted butter

1 medium Spanish onion (about ¾ pound), halved lengthwise and thinly sliced

6 medium garlic cloves, thinly sliced

3 tablespoons Maldon or another flaky sea salt

3½ pounds Yukon Gold potatoes, peeled, cut into ½-inch pieces, and rinsed well

6 cups Simple Chicken Stock (page 245)

FOR FINISHING

2 tablespoons extra-virgin olive oil, plus a healthy drizzle

4 medium garlic cloves, very thinly sliced

A big handful of delicate flat-leaf parsley sprigs, very roughly chopped

Maldon or another flaky sea salt

ing and swirling the pan, until the garlic goes golden brown at the edges, 30 seconds to 1 minute. Add the parsley and a generous pinch of salt, stir, and cook until the parsley wilts and goes a bit crispy, about 1 minute.

Scrape the garlic-parsley mixture into the hot soup. Stir in a healthy drizzle of olive oil and cream, some black pepper, and salt to taste. Haul the pot to the table with a ladle and serve straightaway.

A healthy drizzle of heavy cream

Freshly ground black pepper

top to tail

WHOLE POT-ROASTED CAULIFLOWER WITH TOMATOES AND ANCHOVIES

Many years ago, when I was at The River Café, I saw my mentor Rose Gray cook a head of cauliflower as if it were a hunk of meat. I watched her lift the whole thing out of the pot and slice it into slabs, like a lamb shoulder. When I got stuck in, the dish reminded me of roast dinner, with all the complex flavors and satisfying heft, except without any meat. You can use any old type of cauliflower, though I think the green variety looks especially nice with the red sauce. Even better, find Romanesco cauliflower, with its spiral florets, like a veg from another planet.

Position a rack in the center of the oven and preheat to 450°F.

Put the cauliflower on its side on a cutting board. Trim the base of the stem of any brown bits, if necessary. Remove the core at the bottom as though you were coring a tomato: insert a small sharp knife about 1 inch into the base of the stem, make a circular cut to loosen the core, then pry it out and discard. The core can be tough, plus the hollow allows the heat to penetrate the head while it cooks.

Heat the oil in a heavy oven-safe pot (wide enough to hold the cauliflower with about 3 inches to spare and deep enough to cover with a lid) over medium-high heat until it smokes lightly. Add the cauliflower cored side up and spend 5 minutes or so browning it, using tongs to rotate it and lowering the heat if the browned patches threaten to get too dark. Carefully turn the head over to brown the stem side slightly, about 2 minutes.

Move the cauliflower to one side of the pot (you may transfer it to a plate if your pot isn't quite wide enough, then return it to the pot once you add the tomatoes) and add the garlic, anchovies, and rosemary to the other side. Cook, stirring a bit, until the garlic is light golden

serves 4 to 6 as a side

1 medium head Romanesco, green, or white cauliflower (about 2¼ pounds), all but imperfect stalks and leaves left on

5 tablespoons extra-virgin olive oil, plus a healthy drizzle for finishing

3 medium garlic cloves, thinly sliced

3 salt-packed whole anchovies, soaked and filleted (see page 13)

¾ teaspoon finely chopped rosemary leaves

1 cup drained, trimmed, and coarsely chopped canned whole tomatoes (see page 16)

¼ cup dry white wine, such as Sauvignon Blanc, plus several glugs

3 dried pequín chiles, crumbled, or pinches of red pepper flakes

1 teaspoon Maldon or another flaky sea salt

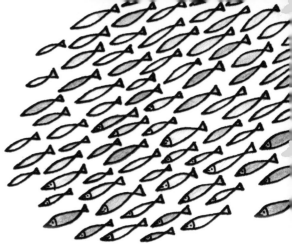

brown, about 30 seconds. Move the cauliflower back into the center, then add the tomatoes, ¼ cup of the wine, the chiles, and the salt. Spend a minute or so stirring, basting, and piling some of the solids onto the cauliflower.

Cover the pot, lower the heat if necessary to maintain a simmer, and cook for 5 minutes or so (just so the tomatoes have a chance to concentrate in flavor). Pop the pot in the oven and roast, basting occasionally, until you can stick a knife into the thickest part of the head with almost no resistance, 45 minutes to 1 hour. Your goal as it roasts is to peek under the lid every 15 minutes or so to check on the sauce. It should be liquidy but still taste punchy and intense, so add a glug of wine whenever it threatens to get too thick.

Carefully transfer the cauliflower head to a plate, cut it in half through the stem or slice it like a roast, and spoon on all the tasty stuff left in the pot. Add a healthy drizzle of olive oil and dig in.

ROASTED CARROTS WITH CARROT-TOP PESTO AND BURRATA

If you can get your hands on burrata—a really special cheese, like delicate mozzarella with a creamy center—then you're already most of the way toward a great dish. In the spring, I'll serve burrata with Snap Pea Salad (page 23); in high summer, I'll pair it with slices of ripe tomato, good olive oil, and flaky salt. When summer fades, I crave burrata with roasted carrots, a pairing that's less common but no less worthy of your attention. The two are like good mates, each helping the other along: the sweetness of the carrots sets off the tanginess of the cheese; the cheese's tanginess makes the carrots tastes even sweeter. Pesto made from the carrot tops adds color and salty, herbaceous wallops throughout the dish.

Position a rack in the center of the oven and preheat to 500°F.

Pour 2 tablespoons of the oil into a heavy ovenproof pan big enough to hold the carrots in a single layer. Set the pan over high heat and bring the oil to a light smoke. Add the carrots, sprinkle on 1 teaspoon of the salt, and turn the carrots to coat them in the oil. Cook, turning over the carrots occasionally, until they're browned in spots, 6 to 8 minutes. Pop the pan in the oven and roast, shaking the pan occasionally, until the carrots are evenly tender, 8 to 12 minutes, depending on the size of your carrots. Let the carrots cool slightly. Halve the burrata and arrange the halves on a platter. Arrange the carrots on the platter so they're pointing this way and that. Add the pesto here and there in little dollops.

Pluck enough 2- to 3-inch delicate sprigs from the reserved carrot tops to make about 1½ lightly packed cups and toss them in a bowl with the basil. Whisk together the remaining 2 tablespoons of the oil with the lemon juice and a good pinch of salt in a small bowl until

serves 4 to 6 as a side

20 small carrots (the size of pointer fingers), scrubbed well but not peeled, all but ½-inch of the tops removed and reserved

4 tablespoons extra-virgin olive oil

1 teaspoon plus a few pinches of Maldon or another flaky sea salt

½ pound room-temperature burrata, drained

About 3 tablespoons Carrot Top Pesto (page 234)

A five-finger pinch of basil leaves, torn at the last minute if large

1 tablespoon lemon juice

the mixture looks creamy. Use a little of the lemon dressing to lightly dress the carrot top–basil mixture, sprinkle on a little more salt, and toss well. Arrange the mixture on top of the carrots and burrata. Drizzle everything with the remaining lemon dressing and serve.

ROASTED WHOLE TOKYO TURNIPS

I can't bear to pass by Tokyo turnips, also called Japanese or Harukei turnips, when I see them at the market. First off, I know that this variety gets especially sweet and juicy when cooked. But almost as important, they're very, very cute. You'd be mad to ignore the greens, of course, and not just because they make up ninety percent of the veg you hauled home, but also because when they go wilty and slightly crispy in the oven they take on an awesome, almost seaweedy flavor. This tangle of turnips and greens makes a perfect appetizer platter, perhaps alongside thinly sliced prosciutto, which you and your mates can go at with your fingers, lifting each nibble by the greens.

Position a rack in the center of the oven and preheat to 425°F. Halve each turnip lengthwise, making sure each half has plenty of stems and leaves attached. Submerge the turnips (greens and all) in a large container of water, gently swishing the greens around with your hands to dislodge any grit. Next, hold the base of the greens of each turnip under running water for a few seconds, gently separating the stems to make sure no grit is hiding out. Drain very well on kitchen towels and pat dry.

Pour 3 tablespoons of the oil into a very wide, heavy ovenproof skillet or enameled baking dish big enough to hold the turnips in a single layer. Set the skillet over medium-high heat and bring the oil to a smoke. (If using a baking dish, it should either straddle two burners or you should rotate it occasionally to make sure it gets even heat.)

Add the turnips cut sides down to the oil in one layer. This is a bit of a puzzle to solve, but it's good fun. You'll probably need to position the turnips so the greens face this way and that and some hang over the sides of the skillet. Cook until the cut sides are light golden brown, 5 to 8 minutes. Sprinkle on the salt and half of the parsley,

serves 4 to 6 as a side

16 Tokyo turnips (each a little smaller than a Ping-Pong ball), all but imperfect roots, stems, and leaves left on

3 tablespoons extra-virgin olive oil, plus a healthy drizzle for finishing

2 teaspoons Maldon or another flaky sea salt

A large handful of delicate flat-leaf parsley sprigs, roughly chopped

About 1 tablespoon red wine vinegar

then tuck all the turnip greens inside the skillet or baking dish and put it in the oven.

Roast, peeking at the cut sides and fluffing up the greens occasionally, until the greens are wilted, tender, and crispy in parts and the turnips are very tender (you should be able to insert a sharp knife with no resistance), 20 to 25 minutes. As you cook, carefully turn over any turnips whose undersides threaten to get darker than golden brown.

Remove the baking dish from the oven. Sprinkle on just enough vinegar so that you can taste its flavor but not its sting and the remaining parsley. Drizzle on some olive oil and sprinkle on more salt, if you fancy. Have a gentle toss and serve straightaway.

SWISS CHARD (LEAVES AND STEMS) WITH MARJORAM

Sometimes I'll do nothing more than boil chard and eat the silky, lemony leaves with just a drizzle of olive oil and a sprinkle of salt. When I want something a little more substantial, I take the extra step of sautéing the boiled chard in oil, adding red onion for its meatiness and garlic for its roasty complexity and the way it rounds off the sharp, acidic edge of the chard. The preparation makes a fine filling for cannelloni (page 137) or a satisfying side dish all by itself.

serves 4 to 6 as a side

Kosher salt

2 pounds green Swiss chard (2 or 3 bunches), stems and leaves separated

¼ cup extra-virgin olive oil

1 medium red onion (about ¾ pound), finely diced

1 teaspoon Maldon or another flaky sea salt

2 medium garlic cloves, sliced

2 five-finger pinches of marjoram leaves

Bring a large pot of water to a boil and add enough kosher salt so it tastes lightly salty. Add the chard leaves and cook just until they're tender and tear very easily, 1 to 2 minutes. Drain the leaves well, let them cool, lightly squeeze them to get rid of some of the water, and roughly chop them.

Heat the oil in a medium pot or Dutch oven over high heat. When the oil shimmers, add the onion and salt, reduce the heat to medium-low, and cook at a steady sizzle, stirring occasionally, until the onion is soft and lightly browned at the edges, 12 to 15 minutes.

Meanwhile, toss the garlic and marjoram together on a cutting board, and chop them very finely until the mixture looks a bit like blue cheese. Add the garlic mixture to the onions, stir, and cook until the garlic is golden brown, about 3 minutes.

While the garlic cooks, trim off any brown bits from the chard stems and thinly slice the stems. When the garlic has browned, add the stems to the pot. Stir, cover, and cook, stirring now and then, until they're fully tender, about 12 minutes. Add the chard leaves to the pot, cover the pot again, and cook, stirring occasionally, for a few minutes just to let the flavors mingle.

Serve hot as a side dish or let cool to room temperature if you're making cannelloni.

BOILED BEETS, STEMS, AND GREENS

When I find beautiful bunches at the market, I use them from nose to tail—or at least from root to leaf. Beet greens are too often discarded. When the greens are pert and unblemished, you'd be mad to ignore them. That'd be as rash as buying a pig and tossing away its ears and feet. I even keep the beet skins on. If beets weren't always served peeled, I think people would cook them more. Keeping the skins on spares you purply hands. The skins taste quite nice, too.

Trim the beet stems to about ½ inch, reserving the rest of the stems and leaves. Leave the beets' spindly roots intact. Cut the stems from the leaves. Keep the leaves whole and cut the stems into 4-inch lengths. You should have about 2 cups of stems and 3 large handfuls of leaves.

Pour 2 inches of water into a medium pot, add the garlic and thyme, and bring the water to a boil over high heat. Season the water with kosher salt so it tastes a little less salty than the sea. Add the beets and boil, stirring occasionally and topping off the water if the level drops below the beets, until the beets are tender but not mushy, about 40 minutes.

Use a slotted spoon to transfer the beets to a mixing bowl. Halve any larger beets through the stem, if you fancy. Add the olive oil, tarragon, shallots, Maldon salt, and vinegar and have a good stir.

Remove and discard the garlic and thyme from the water. Add 3 cups of water to the pot, let it return to the boil, and add the beet stems. Cook, stirring occasionally, until they're tender with a slight bite, about 4 minutes. Use the slotted spoon to transfer the stems to the bowl with the beets.

Add the greens to the water, have a good stir, and cook just until they tear easily, about 3 minutes. Drain the leaves in a colander, let

serves 4 to 6 as a side

20 or so golf-ball-size baby beets with healthy greens

6 medium garlic cloves, unpeeled

6 or so small thyme sprigs

Kosher salt

¼ cup extra-virgin olive oil

A five-finger pinch of tarragon leaves, roughly chopped

1 tablespoon finely chopped shallots

2 teaspoons Maldon or another flaky sea salt

1 teaspoon good, thick balsamic vinegar

them cool to the touch, and gently squeeze them to remove some of the water they've absorbed.

Give the beets and stems another good stir, then use your hands to pile them on a plate. Add the greens to the liquid remaining in the mixing bowl, toss well, then transfer them to the plate as well. Eat straightaway.

satisfying salads

BITTER LEAVES WITH POMEGRANATE AND GRILLED-VEGETABLE VINAIGRETTE

Salads, to me, are about balance and surprise. Here I assemble an array of bitter leaves—some crunchy and others soft, some mild and others bracingly sharp—and toss them with sweet-sour pomegranate seeds and a fluffy grating of salty cheese. The sneaky bits of grilled vegetables in the dressing provide the occasional delight of biting into a meaty chunk of fennel or sweet onion.

I'd happily make this salad with tight round heads of standard radicchio, but to make the salad really special, I look for thrilling varieties like Castelfranco, with its looser speckled heads, or tardivo, whose narrow, sturdy leaves resemble long fingers. And because even the loveliest radicchio can go a bit limp at the market or in the fridge, I'll typically soak the leaves for about 15 minutes in icy water before making the salad.

Combine the radicchio, kale, and endive in a very large mixing bowl. Add the dressing and toss very well with your hands. Make sure you distribute the grilled bits in the dressing and give the leaves a good rub to coat them with the liquidy part of the dressing. Add the pomegranate seeds, have another gentle toss, and transfer the salad to a large shallow bowl or platter. Sprinkle on the pecorino and serve straightaway.

serves 4 to 6 as a side

¾ pound radicchio (preferably a few varieties), root ends trimmed off, separated into individual leaves, and torn into bite-size pieces

1 small bunch Tuscan kale (cavolo nero), thick stems removed, leaves torn into bite-size pieces (about 4 cups, lightly packed)

¼ pound Belgian endive, root end trimmed off, halved crosswise, bottom half sliced, and top half separated into individual leaves

Grilled-Vegetable Vinaigrette (page 236)

¼ cup pomegranate seeds

1 ounce aged pecorino cheese, finely grated on a rasp-style grater

GREEK SALAD

Some of my favorite recipes are those that rely on the little things. Take this version of Greek salad. First, you choose your ingredients carefully—for instance, ripe tomatoes (taut-skinned and unblemished), of course, but also perfect cucumbers (sweet, crisp ones with character; none that are watery or full of big old seeds). Then, have a bit of fun cutting them: using a very sharp knife (this will spare you mushy, ragged-edged tomatoes), cut them into different shapes of similar size, some with sharp angles. These and a few other small details—briefly chilling the tomatoes and cucumbers and quick-pickling the onions—turn a familiar collection of ingredients into a really special salad.

Put the cucumbers and tomatoes in separate bowls and pop them in the fridge just until they're cold, about 30 minutes.

Meanwhile, add the onions to a small bowl. Add the vinegar, 2 tablespoons of the oil, and a healthy pinch of salt, and mix well with your hands. Let the onions sit just until they get pickly, a few minutes.

In a separate small bowl, stir together the remaining 2 tablespoons of oil, the lemon juice, and a good pinch of salt until the mixture looks creamy. Combine the tomatoes and cucumber in one bowl, pour in the lemon dressing, and toss gently but well.

Grab a large platter (or 4 to 6 plates) and make a pretty layer of cucumbers and tomatoes, so the colors and types of the vegetables are well divvied up. Give the onions one more toss, then use your hands to add them (reserving their pickly liquid) here and there over the cucumbers and tomatoes. Scatter on the olives and mint. Use your hands to crumble the feta into pieces large, medium, and small as you scatter it on top. Finally, drizzle on the liquid remaining in the onion bowl. Eat straightaway.

serves 4 to 6 as a side

¾ pound crunchy cucumbers without big seeds (preferably a few varieties), peeled and cut into irregular ¾-inch pieces

Generous 1 pound mixed heirloom tomatoes, halved, cored, trimmed of any pale bits, and cut into irregular 1-inch pieces

¼ pound cherry tomatoes (about ¾ cup), halved through the stem end if large

2 slender spring onions, green tops and root ends trimmed, bulbs cut into ¼-inch-thick rounds and separated into rings (about ½ cup)

2 tablespoons Banyuls vinegar (available at specialty shops and online)

4 tablespoons extra-virgin olive oil

Maldon or another flaky sea salt

1 tablespoon lemon juice

20 or so Niçoise olives, firmly pressed with the flat of a knife and pitted

A five-finger pinch of mint leaves (preferably black mint)

5 ounces creamy feta cheese (preferably goat feta)

SALAD SANDWICHES

Don't tell me you've never had a salad sandwich! When I was a girl, my family practically lived on them come summer, when it was steamy outside and the last thing my mum wanted to do was hunch over a hot stove. The salad sandwich is just what it sounds like: bread piled with stuff like tomatoes, cucumbers, lettuce, and onion. My mum would add spring onions from her garden and slather the bread with butter and Heinz Salad Cream. The ones I make today aren't much different, though I typically make my own version of salad cream and might occasionally add boiled eggs with oozy yolks or use goat cheese butter. Sometimes I'll even bake my own white bread. But really, the little details are up to you.

Fill a medium pot at least halfway with water and bring it to a boil over high heat. Use a slotted spoon to gently add the eggs to the water and cook them for 7 minutes (set a timer), then run them under cold water until they're fully cooled. Lightly tap each egg against the counter to crack the shell all over, then carefully peel them. Slice them however you'd like just before you add them to the sandwich.

Lay the tomato, cucumber, and onion in more or less one layer on a large platter or cutting board. Squeeze a little lemon juice over the veg, then add a good drizzle of olive oil and a sprinkle of salt. Flip them over and rub them gently, just to make sure they're all seasoned.

Spread each slice of bread with butter. Layer the tomato, cucumber, onion, lettuce, salad cream, and eggs on 4 slices of bread: I like to start with the tomatoes, then lettuce, then a good old slather of salad cream, then the eggs, the cucumber, and finally the onion. Top with the remaining bread and give each sandwich a firm but gentle press with your palm. Eat straightaway.

makes 4

4 large eggs

1 pound tomatoes, cut into ¼-inch-thick slices

1 medium crunchy cucumber with minimal seeds, thinly sliced

12 or so rings red onion or 24 or so rings red spring onions

½ lemon

A good drizzle extra-virgin olive oil

Maldon or another flaky sea salt

Eight ¾-inch-thick slices Pullman loaf white bread

A few knobs butter, at room temperature

½ pound Little Gem lettuce (about 2 heads) or another crunchy lettuce, root end and floppy outer leaves discarded, cut into ¼-inch-thick slices

About ½ cup Salad Cream (page 237)

STEAMED AND RAW RADISH SALAD WITH KIMCHI AND SESAME

I'm no Korean mother in the kitchen, but I can't get enough of Korean food. So I thought I'd have a bit of fun with three of my favorite Korean ingredients—sesame, radish, and kimchi. Because I'm an Englishwoman with an Englishwoman's palate, the salad I came up with is a quiet one, not full of the fermented fireworks you might expect from Mum. Because I love radishes so very much, I chose to showcase their sweet, sharp bite in a mellow, mouth-fillingly flavorful sesame dressing. I like that in some bites, however, you do get a hit of spicy, funky kimchi.

Put a steamer insert (or a colander, so long as the pot's lid can still close) in a large pot with a lid. Add about ½ inch water to the pot, pop on the lid, and bring to a boil over high heat. Add the daikon radishes to the insert, cover again, and let them steam until they're fully tender but not mushy, 12 to 15 minutes. Remove the daikon and let it cool. Put the steamed and raw radishes in the fridge to chill for about 15 minutes.

Meanwhile, put the sesame seeds in a small skillet. Set it over medium heat and toast, stirring and tossing frequently, until they're a few shades darker, 3 to 5 minutes. Transfer them to a bowl to cool. Set 1 teaspoon of the seeds aside and pour the rest into a mortar, along with a pinch of salt. Thoroughly pound the seeds, add 1 tablespoon of the neutral oil, and stir until smooth.

Pulse half of the drained kimchi in a small food processor until you have a coarse puree. Transfer it to a bowl and mix in the rest of the kimchi, the kimchi liquid, the sesame oil, the remaining 3 tablespoons of the neutral oil, and 1 teaspoon of salt.

Combine the kimchi mixture, steamed radishes, raw radishes, and Little Gem leaves in a large bowl and toss well. Season to taste with salt and transfer the vegetables to a plate in a heap. Drizzle the sesame paste mixture over the vegetables, then sprinkle on the remaining sesame seeds.

serves 4 to 6 as a side

¾ pound daikon radishes (each no thicker than 1½ inches), peeled, topped, tailed, and cut into 1-inch irregularly shaped pieces

1 pound mixed small radishes (some with pert greens left on), halved lengthwise if larger than 1 inch in diameter

2 tablespoons plus 1 teaspoon sesame seeds

Maldon or another flaky sea salt

4 tablespoons neutral oil, such as safflower or grapeseed

¾ cup roughly chopped drained kimchi (preferably homemade, page 225), plus 2 tablespoons of the kimchi liquid

1 teaspoon toasted sesame oil

1 head Little Gem lettuce, root end and floppy outer leaves discarded, leaves separated

ROASTED CAULIFLOWER AND GRAIN SALAD WITH PISTACHIOS AND POMEGRANATE

When I make salads, I try to make sure every bite keeps the diner interested. Here, that means putting together a bunch of elements—aromatic roasted cauliflower, the snappy grains, the sweet-salty onions, rich pistachios, and tart, crunchy pomegranate seeds—to ensure each mouthful is a bit different from the last. The list of ingredients for this recipe might be lengthy, but I promise this salad isn't hard to make and is well worth the effort it requires. You can simmer the grains—you might even seek out a rice blend like the Lundberg brand's "Jubilee" mix—while the cauliflower is roasting and the onions are getting soft and sweet in a pan. And if you must, you can store the grains, cauliflower, and onions in the fridge overnight and let them come to room temperature before assembling the salad.

Position a rack in the center of the oven and preheat to 450°F.

Combine the raisins and carrot juice in a small bowl and set it aside. Toast the coriander seeds in a small pan over medium-high heat, shaking the pan frequently, until they smell really warm and inviting, 3 to 5 minutes. Grind the seeds to a powder in a spice grinder or pound them in a mortar.

Combine the cauliflower in a large mixing bowl with the garlic, chiles, ¼ cup of the olive oil, 1 heaping teaspoon of the salt, and 2 teaspoons of the ground coriander (reserve the rest for the final step). Toss well to coat the cauliflower in oil and spices and spread the mixture out in a single layer in a large, heavy enameled baking dish. Add ¼ cup of water to the bowl, swish it around to get at any stubborn spices, and pour it into the baking dish (around, not over, the cauliflower).

Cover the dish tightly with foil and pop it into the oven. Cook until the cauliflower is tender with a slight bite and the water is all gone, about

serves 6 as a side

¼ cup golden raisins

¼ cup carrot juice

1 tablespoon coriander seeds

1 medium head cauliflower, trimmed and cut into florets (about 2 x 2 inches)

2 medium garlic cloves, very finely chopped

3 dried pequín chiles, crumbled, or pinches of red pepper flakes

¼ cup plus 5 tablespoons extra-virgin olive oil

Generous 2 teaspoons plus a healthy pinch of Maldon or another flaky sea salt

1 medium red onion (about ½ pound), halved and thinly sliced

2 cups cooked grain, such as freekeh, farro, pearled barley, rye berries, or brown rice

¼ cup unsalted roasted pistachios, coarsely chopped

¼ cup pomegranate seeds

15 minutes. Remove the foil and continue cooking, stirring now and then, until the cauliflower is browned in spots and fully tender but not mushy, about 8 minutes more. Transfer the cauliflower to a plate and let cool to room temperature.

Heat 2 tablespoons of the oil in a medium skillet over medium-high heat until the oil smokes lightly. Add the onion, stir well, and cook, stirring often and near the end scraping the pan frequently so nothing burns, until the onion is very soft, sweet, and dark brown at the edges, about 15 minutes. Add 1 teaspoon of the salt, stir well, and transfer to a large mixing bowl to cool to room temperature.

Add the roasted cauliflower to the cooled onion. Add the cooked grains, pistachios, pomegranate seeds, preserved lemon, lemon juice, remaining 3 tablespoons of oil, the reserved ground coriander, the soaked raisins (including any remaining carrot juice), and a healthy pinch or two of salt.

Toss the mint and parsley together on the cutting board and very coarsely chop them. Add the herbs to the mixing bowl, toss everything gently but well with your hands, and serve.

1 tablespoon finely chopped preserved lemon rind (from 1 very small preserved lemon, flesh and pith discarded)

2 tablespoons lemon juice

A small handful of mint leaves (preferably black mint)

A small handful of delicate flat-leaf parsley sprigs

satisfying salads **89**

BEAN AND MUSHROOM SALAD

This is the sort of salad I'd make at home. It's a bit more refined than your average salad—a few components prepared separately and assembled just before you eat—but still uncomplicated and satisfying enough to serve as a meal for two along with a bit of bread. Feel free to use this recipe as a jumping-off point for your own twist on things. Black trumpets and chanterelles are swell, but so are portobello mushrooms. Canned beans work in a pinch, so long as they're perked up with vinegar and lashed with olive oil. And whatever greens you use, be sure they're good and sturdy, so they can stand up to the warm beans and mushrooms.

cook the mushrooms

Heat about 1 teaspoon of oil (just enough to thinly coat the bottom of the pan) in a large skillet over high heat until it smokes. Add half the mushrooms and cook, stirring frequently, until the mushrooms have wilted and are no longer raw, about 1 minute. Transfer the mushrooms to a bowl, wipe out the pan, add about another teaspoon of oil, and repeat with the remaining mushrooms. Let the skillet cool.

Wipe out the skillet again and set it over high heat. Add the butter, let it melt a bit, then add the garlic and cook, stirring, just until it begins to brown, about 20 seconds. Add the parsley, give the pan a good shake, then add the cooked mushrooms. Cook for a minute, stirring often, then add a healthy pinch of salt, and keep cooking until the mushrooms have a kiss of brown, 1 to 2 minutes more. Take the pan off the heat and squeeze on just enough lemon to add brightness but not acidity. Set the pan aside for the moment.

assemble the salad

Combine the beans and bean liquid, the vinegar, 3 tablespoons of the oil, and ½ teaspoon of salt in a medium skillet. Set it over high heat

serves 4 to 6 as a side

2 teaspoons plus 3 tablespoons extra-virgin olive oil, plus several glugs for the greens

10 ounces mixed yellow foot chanterelle and black trumpet mushrooms, cleaned (see "Cleaning Wild Mushrooms," page 135)

2 tablespoons unsalted butter

1 medium garlic clove, finely chopped

A small handful of delicate flat-leaf parsley sprigs, leaves coarsely chopped, stems thinly sliced

Maldon or another flaky sea salt

1 lemon, halved

1 cup Simple Beans (page 244), plus 1 cup of their tasty liquid

2 teaspoons Banyuls vinegar (available at specialty shops and online)

3 large handfuls of torn sturdy mixed greens and chicories (about ½ pound), such as stemmed Tuscan kale and radicchio

and bring the liquid to a strong simmer, shaking and swirling the pan regularly (if you stir, you risk breaking the beans), until the mixture looks glossy but isn't gloppy, about 5 minutes. Take the pan off the heat.

Toss the greens in a large bowl with a few glugs of olive oil, a healthy squeeze of lemon, and a sprinkle of salt. Transfer them to a platter or large plate, then spoon on the beans and mushrooms here and there.

ROASTED and RAW FENNEL SALAD with BLOOD ORANGE and BOTTARGA

Any time a vegetable is as tasty raw as it is cooked, it's fun to explore combining its different sides in one salad. For example, I'm big on the crunch and perfume of raw fennel. But I also love the way roasting fennel gives it a meaty texture as well as a sweeter, more concentrated, and more complex taste. When you combine the two preparations—along with fennel seeds, pollen, and fronds to add even more layers of flavor—the salad goes from just another nice dish on your table to the meal's main event.

Position a rack in the center of the oven and preheat to 450°F.

Halve two of the fennel bulbs through the root end, then cut them through the root nub (so each wedge stays intact) into approximately 1-inch-thick wedges. Combine the wedges in a mixing bowl with the garlic, fennel seeds, chiles, ¼ cup of the oil, ½ teaspoon of the salt, and ¼ cup of water, and toss well. Spread the mixture in a heavy enameled baking dish (large enough to hold the fennel in a single layer with a little room to spare) and cover tightly with foil. Roast the fennel until it is tender (it should meet with almost no resistance when poked with a knife) and golden brown on the bottom, 25 to 30 minutes. Remove the foil and roast just until the golden brown color gets a shade or so darker, 3 to 5 minutes more. Let the fennel cool to room temperature.

Meanwhile, halve one of the oranges and squeeze 3 tablespoons of juice into a small bowl. Use a sharp knife to cut off just enough of the top and bottom of the remaining oranges to expose a full circle of the flesh on either side. Stand them on a flat end, and cut along the border where the flesh meets the pith, following the curve of the fruit to remove the pith and peel. Repeat the process until all you have left are nice round, naked fruits. If you've missed any white pith, trim it off. Slice the fruit crosswise into ¼- to ⅜-inch-thick rounds. Flick out any seeds.

serves 4 to 6 as a side

4 large fennel bulbs, stalks and outermost layer discarded, tender fronds reserved, root end trimmed of brown bits

2 medium garlic cloves, finely chopped

½ teaspoon fennel seeds, coarsely crushed in a mortar

3 dried pequín chiles, crumbled, or pinches of red pepper flakes

¼ cup plus 2 tablespoons extra-virgin olive oil

1½ teaspoons Maldon or another flaky sea salt

4 blood oranges

1 tablespoon lemon juice

Several turns of freshly ground black pepper

A handful of delicate, peppery arugula

¼ cup unsalted roasted pistachios, very coarsely crushed

1 teaspoon fennel pollen

1 ounce *bottarga di muggine* (salted mullet roe), finely grated on a rasp-style grater

To the blood orange juice in the bowl, whisk in the lemon juice, the pepper, the remaining 2 tablespoons of oil, and 1 teaspoon of salt.

Slice the remaining 2 fennel bulbs crosswise into ¼-inch-thick slices (only remove the core if it's very tough) and separate the layers with your fingers. Toss the raw fennel, roasted fennel (and any oil and browned bits left in the pan), and dressing in a large mixing bowl. Use your hands to give it all a gentle scrunch—just to help the flavors come together.

Very coarsely chop enough of the reserved fennel fronds to give you a handful. Add the fronds, arugula, and pistachios to the bowl, and toss again.

Spoon some of the fennel mixture onto a platter, arrange some blood orange slices here and there, then add another layer of fennel and oranges. Sprinkle on the fennel pollen, bottarga, and if you'd like, a healthy pinch of salt. Serve straightaway.

simple things
fennel

I suppose boiled fennel doesn't sound all that appetizing. It's true, raw fennel has a fantastic crunch, entrancing perfume, and delicate, feminine sweetness. But after it's had a nice bath in salty boiling water, it goes subtle, creamy, and a bit juicy. And that's my favorite way to eat the veg.

Next time you come across some—I like the especially bulbous variety called Florence fennel, and don't care for baby fennel—grab a few bulbs and get to work. Bring plenty of water to a boil and add to it a good handful of kosher salt. The water should taste quite salty, though not as salty as the sea. The bigger your bulbs, the more heavily you should salt your water. Remove the stalks and tough outer layer of the fennel and consider saving them for stock. Trim any brown bits from the root end, but keep the root intact. Halve the bulbs through the root and plunk them in the water. They're ready when you can cut them with a spoon.

While the fennel cooks, take some of the feathery fronds—from the center of the cluster, where they're especially sweet—and coarsely chop them. Drain the fennel, pat it dry, arrange it on a plate, and season with flaky sea salt, a little crumbled dried chile, a light drizzle of good olive oil, and a few drops of lemon juice—just to add a bit of brightness. Finish the dish by sprinkling on the fronds—they add back a little of that fresh sweet flavor the boiling stole.

summer, lovely summer

IF-IT-AIN'T-BROKE EGGPLANT CAPONATA

I learned to make caponata at The River Café in London, and as with many things I learned to make there, their version became the one to which I aspire whenever I make caponata today. Before The River Café, I had a problem with caponata. I'm not big on the raisins that wind up in so many renditions. I don't like the common addition of sugar, either—the artificial sweetness makes me shudder. But Rose and Ruth turned to ripe tomatoes and slowly cooked onion and celery for natural and more complex sweetness. Rather than a ton of vinegar, they found brightness in just a touch of it along with celery leaves and olives. And they taught me one of those kitchen tricks that can change how you see an ingredient—before cooking the eggplant, I learned to salt it and then drain off some of its liquid. The magical result? It doesn't absorb nearly as much oil when it cooks. The pieces of eggplant turn out creamy, rather than greasy and mushy. All in all, I barely tinker with their recipe. Why fix what isn't broken?

Toss the eggplant and kosher salt together in a colander and set the colander over a bowl. Let the eggplant sit for about 30 minutes.

Meanwhile, quarter the tomatoes and trim off any pale bits. Hold each chunk over a bowl, and use your fingers to push out the juice and seeds. Strain the juice, discarding the seeds. Finely chop the tomatoes.

Heat 3 tablespoons of the oil in a medium pot over medium-high heat until it shimmers. Add the onion, celery, garlic, and 1 teaspoon of the Maldon salt. Cook, stirring and scraping occasionally, until the onion is translucent and begins to stick to the pot, about 10 minutes. Lower the heat to medium and cook the vegetables for another 10 minutes. Add the chiles and keep cooking, stirring and scraping occasionally, until the vegetables are light brown, soft, and sweet, about 10 minutes more. Stir in the tomatoes and their strained juice and let the mixture simmer, stirring now and then, for about 15 minutes.

serves 6 to 8 as a side

2 pounds large eggplants (preferably a purple variety such as Rosa Bianca), unpeeled, topped, tailed, and cut into about 1½-inch pieces

½ tablespoon kosher salt

1 pound tomatoes, peeled (see page 16) and cored

½ cup plus 3 tablespoons extra-virgin olive oil

1 medium Spanish onion (about ½ pound), finely chopped

1¼ pounds celery, bottoms trimmed, stalks cut into ½-inch irregularly shaped pieces (generous 2 cups), inner leaves reserved and roughly chopped

3 medium garlic cloves, thinly sliced

Maldon or another flaky sea salt

4 dried pequín chiles, crumbled, or pinches of red pepper flakes

1 tablespoon red wine vinegar

Pat the eggplant dry. Heat the remaining ½ cup of olive oil in a medium heavy skillet over medium heat until it shimmers. Cook the eggplant in two batches to avoid crowding the pan, turning the pieces often and adjusting the heat if necessary, until they're deep golden brown on the outside and creamy inside, 10 to 12 minutes per batch. Put the eggplant on paper towels to drain. Let it cool to warm.

Transfer the eggplant to a large bowl, sprinkle with the vinegar and a pinch or two of Maldon salt, and give a very light stir, being careful not to smoosh the pieces. To the bowl, add the tomato mixture, olives, pine nuts, capers, basil, and a small handful of the reserved celery leaves. Have another gentle stir, and season to taste with Maldon salt.

The caponata will keep in an airtight container in the fridge for up to 3 days, but you should always serve it at room temperature.

¼ cup Niçoise olives (or a mixture of varieties), smashed with the flat of a knife, pits removed, and very roughly chopped

¼ cup pine nuts, lightly toasted

2 tablespoons drained capers, roughly chopped

A five-finger pinch of basil leaves, roughly chopped at the last minute

EGGS IN PIPÉRADE

Pipérade is Basque cooking as its simplest. Little more than tomatoes, onions, and peppers cooked together in olive oil, the dish relies on good ingredients and a careful cook. Peeling the peppers allows them to develop a meaty texture. Scraping off the sweet bits of onions and pepper that cling to the pot means they'll never go too dark and turn bitter. The addition of eggs turns it from sauce to a one-pot meal. You may prefer to scramble the eggs with the pipérade or perhaps make an omelet and spoon some of it on top. I like to crack the eggs straight into the pot and let them cook just until the whites have set and the yolks are still good and runny. Whatever way you choose, don't eat this without plenty of toast for mopping up that sauce.

Peel the skin from the peppers using a vegetable peeler and a gentle sawing motion. Slice the peppers into long strips that are somewhere between ¼ and ½ inch thick. Set them aside.

Heat the ¼ cup of oil in a large Dutch oven or heavy skillet over medium heat until it shimmers. Add the onion and 1 teaspoon of the salt. Cook, stirring occasionally, until the onion has softened, about 5 minutes. Push the onion to one side of the pot and add the garlic to the oil. Cook, stirring the garlic occasionally but not the onions, until the garlic turns light golden and smells toasty, about 3 minutes. Stir it all together and cook, stirring now and then, until the onion is lightly browned and very soft, 6 to 8 minutes.

Add the peppers to the pot along with the remaining 1 teaspoon of the salt and cook, stirring often and scraping the bottom after a while, until the onions start to disintegrate and the peppers are tender but not at all mushy, about 10 minutes.

Reduce the heat to medium-low and keep cooking, stirring and scraping, until the pot gets lovely brown sticky stuff on it and the peppers get a bit softer, about 5 minutes more. Have a taste. The peppers

serves 2 as a main

2 pounds mixed yellow and red bell peppers (about 4 medium), halved lengthwise, seeded and deribbed

¼ cup extra-virgin olive oil, plus a healthy drizzle for finishing

1 medium red onion (about ½ pound), halved and thinly sliced

2 teaspoons Maldon or another flaky sea salt

2 medium garlic cloves, thinly sliced

1 cup Simple Tomato Sauce (page 242), at room temperature

A five-finger pinch of basil leaves, roughly chopped, plus more for finishing

3 large eggs

5 dried pequín chiles, crumbled, or pinches of red pepper flakes

should be really sweet and have a meaty texture. Stir in the tomato sauce and cook at a good sizzle until it thickens slightly, a few minutes. Stir in ½ cup of water and the basil and let the mixture return to a simmer. Season to taste with salt.

Add the eggs to the pot, cover with a lid, and reduce the heat to low. Cook until the eggs are to your liking, 4 to 5 minutes for nice runny yolks. Sprinkle the chiles on the yolks, scatter on the rest of the basil, drizzle on some olive oil, and serve straightaway.

PIEDMONTESE PEPPERS WITH TOMATO, BASIL, AND ANCHOVY

The clever cooking method is just one reason to love so-called Piedmontese peppers. Halved bell peppers act as little tubs that hold a whole tomato, an anchovy fillet, a basil leaf, and a few slivers of garlic. As the peppers roast, the tomatoes nesting inside them release a bit of juice, transforming the peppers into hot tubs. The main reason, though, is the result: next thing you know, the flesh of the peppers is creamy and their edges are toasty. The tomatoes' flavor becomes concentrated, and their anchovy-infused juice is sweet, aromatic, and full of umami. I'd happily eat these as is, but you could serve them with some mozzarella or burrata on the side, bread spread with pesto, or alongside lightly dressed arugula.

You want to find tomatoes that are small enough to fit inside the pepper halves but large enough that they rise above the sides. Of course, you can cut larger tomatoes to fit, adding them rounded side up, though the dish will look a little less sexy.

Position a rack in the center of the oven and preheat to 450°F.

Find a heavy enameled baking dish that will fit the peppers snugly and arrange them cut sides up. To each half, add 2 or 3 slices of garlic, an anchovy fillet, a basil leaf, and finally a tomato.

Sprinkle on the salt, add several grindings of pepper, and evenly drizzle the olive oil over everything. Pop the dish in the oven and cook until the edges of the peppers go wrinkly and a bit toasty and the flesh is creamy, 45 minutes to 1 hour. After 20 minutes and every 10 minutes or so thereafter, give the tomatoes a gentle press with the back of a spoon so a little juice squeezes out, then baste the peppers.

Remove the peppers from the oven and let them rest in the baking dish until they're just a bit warmer than room temperature. Baste them once more, then carefully transfer the peppers to plates or a platter, drizzle on the liquid remaining in the pan, and sprinkle on the torn basil.

serves 6 to 8 as a side

8 small red bell peppers (about 2½ pounds), halved lengthwise, seeded and deribbed, green stem nubs left intact

3 medium garlic cloves, thinly sliced

8 salt-packed whole anchovies, soaked and filleted (see page 13)

16 large basil leaves, plus extra, torn, for finishing

16 small to medium tomatoes (about 2 pounds), peeled (see page 16) and cored

1 tablespoon Maldon or another flaky sea salt

Freshly ground black pepper

A healthy drizzle of extra-virgin olive oil

simple things
tomatoes

I love a good tomato table, the spread a proud farmer sets out at her market stand. I love reading the eccentric names of the varieties scribbled on scraps of paper: Striped German, Green Zebra, Brandywine, Cherokee Purple. Some people have a favorite variety, but I like them all. So how do I decide what to buy on any given day? I start by inspecting all the tomatoes and choosing whichever ones are heavy and firm with a slight give. From those I pick the most vividly colored tomatoes, and from those I choose ones where the color (or mottling, in the case of certain heirloom varieties) is the same everywhere, even near the eye, where lesser tomatoes are often pale.

Once at home, I don't do much at all to them. A sprinkle of flaky sea salt. Perhaps a drizzle of olive oil and a few shreds of torn basil. A squeeze of lemon if the tomatoes are quite sweet. My mood determines the way I slice them. If I'm relaxed, I choose thin slices, which give the tomatoes a silky texture as they sort of glide over your tongue. If I'm eager to shove them in my gob, I chop them into good old chunks. They're nice and meaty that way. Either way, a sharp knife is essential: a dull knife will make ragged cuts or even worse, mush the tomatoes.

SUMMERY RIBOLLITA

This classic Tuscan soup is the result of clever cooks who stretched leftover minestrone by adding stale bread. They brought the whole mess to a boil (*ribollita* means "re-boiled" in Italian) and the bread melted, thickening the broth and turning something unassuming into something special. Nowadays, cooks like me have come to love ribollita so much they make it from scratch. Like most simple dishes, it takes a bit of care to get right. The steps are not meant to torment you, I promise. Each has a purpose that you'll taste in the final product. The vegetables must be chopped nice and small, so they'll almost disappear into the soup, and they must be cooked slowly and lovingly to guarantee the soup's complex flavor. You must use beans you've cooked yourself, because their flavorful cooking liquid takes the place of stock. Sweet summer tomatoes must be passed through a food mill to add silkiness. (Well, "must" is a strong word.) At the end of summer, you might decide to swap out chard for another delicate, herbaceous leaf like borage, which gardeners often plant between tomatoes to ward off pests. As the weather turns cold, and you crave an even heartier soup, you might add kale instead of chard and top-notch canned tomatoes instead of fresh. You might also take the onions, carrots, and celery past light brown into deeper, darker territory.

Combine the whole garlic cloves and marjoram on a cutting board and finely chop together until the mixture looks a bit like blue cheese.

Heat ½ cup of the oil in a large pot over medium-high heat until it shimmers. Add the onion, celery, carrot, chard stems, and 1 teaspoon of the salt. Cook, stirring often, for 15 minutes, then stir in the marjoram mixture and the chiles. Reduce the heat to medium-low and cook, stirring often near the end, until the vegetables are very soft, lightly browned, and sweet, about 45 minutes.

Meanwhile, pour just enough water into a medium pot to barely cover the bottom. Bring it to a boil, add the chard leaves, and pop on a lid. Cook, stirring once, until the leaves are fully wilted and ten-

serves 4 as a main

6 medium garlic cloves, peeled, 4 whole, 2 thinly sliced

A small handful of marjoram leaves

½ cup plus 3 tablespoons extra-virgin olive oil, plus a few glugs for finishing

1 medium-large Spanish onion (about ¾ pound), finely diced

4 large celery stalks, finely diced (about 2 cups)

1 large carrot, peeled and finely diced (about 1½ cups)

1 pound Swiss chard (about 1 bunch), leaves separated from the stalks, stalks finely diced, leaves torn into large pieces (about 2¼ cups stems and 5 cups leaves)

2 teaspoons Maldon salt or another flaky sea salt

3 dried pequín chiles, crumbled, or pinches of red pepper flakes, plus more for finishing

2 pounds cherry tomatoes, each pricked with the tip of a sharp knife

der, about 3 minutes. Drain the chard well and give it a rough chop. Wipe out the pot.

Combine the remaining 3 tablespoons of oil and the thinly sliced garlic in the pot. Set the pot over high heat and cook, stirring, until the garlic turns light golden brown, about 1 minute. Add the tomatoes and remaining 1 teaspoon of salt, then cover the pot and lower the heat to medium. Cook, stirring once or twice, until the tomatoes soften and the skins begin to burst, about 8 minutes. Uncover and mash the tomatoes for a couple of minutes.

Pass the tomato mixture through a food mill into a bowl (or if you must, pass it through a mesh strainer set over the bowl, smooshing and stirring to get as much liquid as you can). Discard the solids. You should have about 2 cups of tomato liquid.

Stir the tomato liquid into the pot with the onions, bring it to a simmer over medium heat, and cook for 5 minutes. Add just the beans (reserving the liquid) and continue simmering, stirring occasionally, for a few minutes, just so the ingredients all get to know one another. Stir in the bean liquid, let it come to a simmer, then add the bread to the liquid in one layer. Cook for another 5 minutes or so until the bread begins to melt. Add the chard leaves and stir roughly to help the bread fully melt and thicken the soup. Cook just until the soup is warmed through. If you'd like, add more crumbled chiles, salt, and a few good glugs of olive oil. Serve straightaway.

2½ cups Simple Beans (page 244), including 2½ cups of their tasty liquid

Scant ½ pound slightly stale rustic bread, such as filone, crust discarded, pulled into about 1-inch pieces (about 2 cups)

STEWED ZUCCHINI WITH BASIL

This dish was inspired by a trip to Rome. After a few days, I was tired of cappuccino and, like a proper Englishwoman, desperate for a cup of tea. (A bit lame, I know.) I popped into a tea shop near the Spanish Steps and ordered a pot. Along with the tea I was served a complimentary snack that turned out to be just about the best thing in the world. The waitress had brought over an English muffin (or as we call them in England, muffins) topped with mozzarella and stewed zucchini. It was the simplest thing, this zucchini: soft chunks coated by a little of the creamy smashed vegetable. It was even made with my favorite variety, Romanesco zucchini, which has ridges, speckles, and an earthy quality—a tiny bit like manure, if you ask me.

My version of the dish requires little more than nice zucchini, the kind that are the size of pickling cucumbers, not the fat watery, seedy ones or pinky-size baby ones. Cutting the zucchini into pieces with especially sharp edges means most stay whole, but some break down and coat the others. When summer winds down, I like a little color on the zucchini to give it a warmness and meatiness, as in this recipe. But when the weather's still hot, I prefer none, so I add the salt with the zucchini, to draw out its water sooner. It's really up to you, though.

Cut the zucchini like so: Start by cutting a piece on the diagonal that's about 1 inch long. Turn the zucchini about 45 degrees toward you and cut another piece at the same angle. Return the zucchini to its original position, cut at the same angle, and so on.

Heat the oil in a medium pot (one with high sides that's wide enough to hold the zucchini snugly in about two layers) over high heat until it lightly smokes. Add the zucchini, carve out a little space in the pot, and add the garlic. Don't stir just yet. Cook until the garlic is golden and the zucchini pieces on the bottom are golden brown, 3 to 5 minutes. (If the garlic is done early, pop it on top of the zucchini.) Have a good stir.

serves 4 as a side

1½ pounds small zucchini, topped, tailed, and halved lengthwise

¼ cup extra-virgin olive oil

5 medium garlic cloves, halved lengthwise

1½ teaspoons Maldon or another flaky sea salt

A five-finger pinch of basil leaves, roughly chopped

1 teaspoon lemon juice

½ teaspoon finely grated lemon zest

A few dried pequin chiles, crumbled, or pinches of red pepper flakes (optional)

Sprinkle on ½ teaspoon of the salt, reduce the heat to medium-low, and pop on the lid. Cook, stirring occasionally, for 5 minutes or so. Now, take a listen: if you hear the zucchini frying in oil rather than simmering in a little liquid, then add 2 tablespoons of water. Pop on the lid again and cook, stirring occasionally, until some of the zucchini pieces are tender but not mushy and some are nearly tender, 3 to 5 minutes more.

Stir in the remaining 1 teaspoon of salt and the basil. Cook, without the lid, and every 30 seconds or so use a sturdy whisk or wooden spoon to very roughly stir and strike the zucchini, not to smash the pieces but just to knock off some of the points that have gotten soft. Keep at it until some of the softer pieces have broken down and turned creamy and the other pieces are tender with a slight bite, about 3 minutes. Stir in the lemon juice, zest, chiles, and more salt if you fancy. Eat straightaway.

ZUCCHINI BREAD

Carrot cake and pumpkin pie make a strong case for crafting dessert out of vegetables. Unlike carrots and pumpkins, which are quite sugary, zucchini is only subtly sweet. This makes me wonder who first thought to turn it into a bread that you eat for pudding. Well, whoever did is a clever one indeed. Somehow the zucchini keeps the bread moist and, just as carrots do in cake, provides just a smidgen of its earthy character. My zucchini bread includes the brightness of lemon zest, chunks of walnuts, and a little crunchy topping of sugar. A slice (or two) is just the thing with a cup of milky English breakfast tea hot enough to just barely scald the back of your throat.

Position a rack in the center of the oven and preheat to 350°F. Coat two 9 x 5-inch loaf pans with cooking spray. Cut 2 strips of parchment paper that are the width of the bottom of the loaf pan and twice as long. Lay a parchment paper strip in each loaf pan so it completely covers the bottom and hangs over the pan's two short sides.

Spread the walnuts in a single layer on a baking sheet and bake, stirring occasionally, until they're aromatic but not colored, 6 to 8 minutes. Keep the oven on. Transfer the walnuts to a cutting board to cool, then roughly chop them so you have a mixture of small and large chunks.

Combine the flour, baking soda, baking powder, and cinnamon in a large bowl and stir well. Give both zucchinis a light squeeze with your hands to remove excess surface moisture, lay them on a towel, and give them a light pat.

Put the eggs in the bowl of the stand mixer fitted with the paddle attachment and mix on medium speed, gradually adding the granulated sugar and occasionally scraping the sides of the bowl, until the mixture doubles in volume, turns pale, and looks like a ribbon as it falls when you lift the paddle, about 5 minutes.

Next, with the mixer running on low speed, add the oil in a slow, steady stream, then add the zucchini, vanilla extract, and lemon zest

makes two 9-inch loaves

SPECIAL EQUIPMENT

Two 9 x 5-inch loaf pans, a stand mixer with paddle attachment, and a wire rack

1 cup walnuts (about 3½ ounces)

2 cups all-purpose flour

1½ teaspoons baking soda

¼ teaspoon baking powder

2 teaspoons ground cinnamon

1½ cups coarsely grated green zucchini (grated on the largest holes of a box grater)

1½ cups coarsely grated yellow zucchini (grated on the largest holes of a box grater)

3 large eggs

2 cups granulated sugar

½ cup sunflower or vegetable oil

2 teaspoons vanilla extract

Finely grated zest of 1 large lemon

A five-finger pinch of summer savory leaves (optional)

Large pinch of Maldon or another flaky sea salt

1 tablespoon demerara sugar

and mix until everything is well combined. Turn off the mixer. Add half the flour mixture to the mixer and mix on low speed until almost incorporated. Turn off the mixer, add the remaining flour mixture and walnuts, then mix again on low speed just until incorporated. Mix too much and the bread will be too dense.

Divide the batter evenly between the two loaf pans. Sprinkle the salt and demerara sugar evenly over the surface of the batter. Bake the loaves until a toothpick inserted into the center comes out clean, 50 minutes to 1 hour.

Transfer the pans to a wire rack to cool slightly, about 30 minutes, then use the parchment paper overhang to remove the loaves from the pan, running a knife along the edges of the bread if need be. Put the loaves on a wire rack to cool fully.

Wrapped in plastic wrap, the bread keeps at room temperature for up to 3 days and in the fridge for up to 1 week.

CORN SOUP WITH CREAM AND CHANTERELLE MUSHROOMS

The key to corn soup is finding the sweetest ears you can and then making sure you use every bit of flavor they contain. That means not just slicing the kernels away from the cobs, but also—and this is a really joyful activity—scraping the back of your knife blade down the naked cobs, almost like you're scaling a fish. This gives you a pile of sweet, starchy scrapings that'll add body and flavor to your soup. Then steeping the cobs in the milk and cream means even the dairy gets infused with the corn's essence. For a touch of elegance and to balance all that sweet corn flavor, I top each bowl with sautéed chanterelle mushrooms.

make the soup

Cut the corn kernels from the cobs and measure out 6 cups of kernels. Use the back of the knife blade to scrape each cob of any bits of kernel left behind. Combine the kernels and scrapings in a bowl, reserving the cobs.

Cut the cobs crosswise into a few pieces and pop them into a medium pot along with the milk and cream. Cover the pot, bring to a boil over high heat, then remove the pot from the heat and let it sit, covered, for at least 5 minutes. Remove the cobs, gently scraping them with a spoon to get at any liquid that may be hiding in them, and discard the cobs.

Melt the butter in a large pot over low heat. When the butter froths, add the shallots and salt, stir, and cover the pot. Cook, stirring now and then, until the shallots are soft and creamy but not colored, 10 to 12 minutes. Add the corn kernels and scrapings to the pot and stir. Increase the heat to medium, cover the pot, and cook, stirring occasionally, until the kernels are tender but still have a pop, about 10 minutes.

Add the milk mixture to the pot and give everything a stir. Cover and simmer gently over medium-low heat for another 15 minutes to fully

serves 6 to 8

FOR THE SOUP

8 medium ears corn, shucked

3 cups whole milk

1 cup heavy cream

6 tablespoons unsalted butter

2 large shallots (about ¼ pound), thinly sliced

1 tablespoon Maldon or another flaky sea salt

FOR THE GARNISH

4 tablespoons (½ stick) unsalted butter

6 ounces fresh small golden chanterelle mushrooms, cleaned (see "Cleaning Wild Mushrooms," page 135) and halved through the stem if wider than a nickel

½ teaspoon Maldon or another flaky sea salt

½ lemon

2 tablespoons thinly sliced chives

A healthy drizzle of extra-virgin olive oil

soften the kernels and infuse the liquid with corn flavor. Pour the soup into a large mixing bowl. Working in batches, blend the mixture (be careful when blending hot liquids) until very smooth, adding each batch back to the pot. Keep the soup warm over very low heat for the moment.

prepare the garnish

Melt the butter in a medium skillet over medium-low heat. When the butter froths, add the mushrooms and salt, have a stir, then cover the skillet. Cook the mushrooms, stirring occasionally, just until they're tender and their liquid has melded with the butter to make a simple pan sauce, about 5 minutes. Gently squeeze on just enough lemon juice so that when you taste a chanterelle, you taste its earthy flavor first and a pop of acidity second.

Ladle the soup into bowls. Top each with a spoonful of mushrooms, a drizzle of the pan sauce, a sprinkle of chives, and a drizzle of olive oil. Serve straightaway.

CORN PUDDING

I figure that calling this dish corn pudding, even though some might call it soufflé, will encourage any home cooks put off by soufflé's reputation for being difficult. The recipe certainly isn't. So long as you use the sweetest corn you can find and make sure you're gentle with your fluffy egg whites, then you'll have a pudding that puffs up in golden brown patches so stunningly that your mates might mention that the pudding reminds them of a soufflé. Just smile and nod.

Position a rack in the center of the oven and preheat to 400°F.

Cut the corn kernels from the cobs. Use the back of the knife blade to scrape each cob of any bits of kernel left behind. Transfer the kernels and scrapings to a small pot. Discard the cobs.

Add the cream and milk to the pot and bring the liquid to a boil over medium-high heat. Lower the heat to maintain a gentle simmer and cook until the kernels are tender with a slight bite, about 3 minutes. Stir in the salt. Transfer about half the mixture to a blender and puree until very smooth. Add the remaining corn mixture to the blender and stir well.

Clean the pot and set it over medium-low heat. Add the butter and let it melt and froth a little, then add the flour, whisking until the mixture is fully smooth. Cook, stirring constantly, for a minute or so, so the flour loses its raw flavor. Increase the heat to medium, gradually add the corn mixture, a ladleful at a time, stirring constantly and letting the mixture come to a simmer before adding the next ladleful. Let the mixture cool fully. (If you'd like, speed up the cooling by transferring the mixture to a medium bowl, nesting that bowl in a larger one half filled with very icy water, and stirring frequently.) Thoroughly whisk in the egg yolks.

Generously butter the inside of a 1½-quart, 2-inch-deep round or oval baking dish. Beat the egg whites to stiff peaks in a stainless steel bowl, then carefully use a stainless steel spoon to tenderly fold the whites

serves 4 to 6 as a side

SPECIAL EQUIPMENT
A 1½-quart, 2-inch-deep round or oval baking dish

3 large ears corn, shucked

1 cup heavy cream

½ cup whole milk

1½ tablespoons Maldon or another flaky sea salt

3 tablespoons unsalted butter, at room temperature, cut into several pieces, plus more for the baking dish

2 tablespoons all-purpose flour

4 large eggs, yolks and whites separated

into the corn mixture. You don't want to lose too much of the air you beat into the whites by stirring too much or too roughly. It's fine if you still see streaks of egg whites. Gently scrape it all into the baking dish.

Put the baking dish in a larger baking dish or roasting pan and put it on the oven rack. Carefully pour enough hot water into the larger dish to reach three-quarters of the way up the sides of the smaller dish. Bake, covering loosely with foil after 30 minutes or so if the top is threatening to get dark brown, until the pudding puffs up in golden and golden-brown patches and is just set but still jiggly in the center, 45 to 55 minutes. Let it cool in the water bath just until you can remove the dish with your hands. Serve while it's still warm.

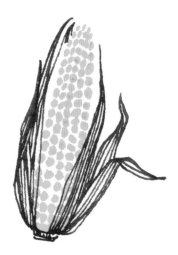

vegetable pastas, polenta, pastries, and friends

FRESH EGG PASTA

When you've made your own pasta, you don't have to do much else to arrive somewhere delicious. Just some butter, black pepper, and a touch of cream would make me happy. Yet fresh pasta is also a fantastic way to make use of the season's bounty. In the spring when asparagus has at last arrived, I add juicy boiled slivers to noodles and sauce it all with luxurious *fonduta* (see page 133). When fall comes and with it chanterelles, I look to pasta to transform them (see page 134) into dinner.

If you haven't yet had a go at making pasta yourself, you're in for a treat. Not only will you be surprised that you can produce such delicate noodles at home, but if you're anything like me you'll also find yourself enjoying the process—the gratifying exertion of kneading the dough until it's as smooth as a baby's bum, the satisfaction of watching the blob of dough become thin sheets as you feed it through a pasta roller. Speaking of rollers, I don't love using electric ones to roll out pasta. Once you start feeding the machine, the rolling happens quite quickly, which puts you under a lot of pressure. I prefer a hand-crank device, which lets you go at your own pace.

Everyone has her own preferences for pasta. I like mine quite eggy, with lots of yolks providing richness and a beautiful yellow color. And I like a mixture of especially fine "00" flour and semolina, which strikes the right balance of texture between silkiness and chewiness. When you're measuring your flour, I suggest using weight instead of volume, because it's more precise: Somehow, no matter how well you've fluffed your flour, a volume measure of 1 cup will almost always yield a slightly different amount.

make the dough

Combine the flours and salt in a large bowl and stir well. Pour the mixture onto a clean work surface, make it into a mound, and use a spoon or your fingers to carve out a big well in the center that's big enough to hold the whole egg and egg yolks. Add the egg and yolks to the well.

**makes about
1¼ pounds**

SPECIAL EQUIPMENT

A hand-cranked pasta machine or a stand mixer with a pasta-roller attachment

6½ ounces (about 1 cup) fine semolina flour, plus more for dusting

6½ ounces (about 1 cup) "00" or "doppio zero" flour, plus more for dusting

⅛ teaspoon kosher salt

1 large egg

12 large egg yolks

Use a fork, holding the tines parallel to your work surface, to break the yolks and stir the eggs in a circular motion. As you stir, you'll see flour from the walls of your well tumbling into the egg. Keep stirring, gradually incorporating the flour into the eggs and occasionally gathering the border of flour closer to the slowly expanding bright yellow center. After 4 minutes or so, you should have a very wet dough surrounded by flour. Now use your hands or a dough scraper to slowly incorporate the rest of the flour, folding and pressing until it's all incorporated.

Cut the dough in half. Knead one piece at a time, keeping the other wrapped in plastic, by pressing firmly down and forward with your palm (one hand on top of the other for force), then folding the dough back onto itself, pushing down and forward again, and turning the dough and doing it all over. Keep at it until the dough is smooth like a baby's bum, 5 to 7 minutes. Kneading will prove more challenging as you work the gluten, so you might occasionally switch to the other piece of dough, wrapping the one you're not kneading in plastic and letting it relax a bit. Wrap each half in plastic wrap and let them rest for at least 20 minutes or up to 1 hour.

roll out the pasta

Cut each piece of dough in half, rolling out one and keeping the other pieces you aren't working with wrapped in plastic wrap. (As you get more comfortable with the process, you might not need to halve them.)

Work with one piece of dough at a time. Form the dough into a rough rectangle that's about 4 x 6 inches. Set the rollers to the widest setting and feed the dough through twice. (If the dough feels at all sticky or doesn't come cleanly from the machine, dust it with a little flour.) Set the rollers to their second widest setting and feed the dough through once. Continue in this manner until the dough has been

through each setting once. This process works the gluten in the dough, giving the pasta a lovely texture. At this point, it's fine if the long sheet of dough looks ragged or uneven.

Fold the sheet of pasta onto itself several times to form a rough rectangle (about 5 x 8 inches) and press firmly with your hands so the layers stick together. Set the rollers to the widest setting again. Feed the dough through once at each setting until you reach about halfway to the narrowest one. Then start feeding the dough through twice at each setting, continuing toward the narrowest one, until your dough is about 6 x 36 inches and about 1 millimeter thick. Cover the dough with a damp towel and repeat with the remaining dough.

for tagliatelle Cut the long sheets crosswise into smaller, shorter sections that are as long as you'd like your pasta to be. I like my tagliatelle to be 12 to 15 inches long. Dust each side with semolina, giving the dough a light rub, and stack the sheets neatly. Cut the stack lengthwise into ½-inch-wide slices. Gently toss the slices, separating them into individual noodles as you do.

for pappardelle Follow the instructions for tagliatelle, but cut the stack into 1-inch-wide slices.

for cannelloni Cut the sheets into roughly 4 x 6-inch rectangles. There's no need to make perfect rectangles.

At this point the pasta is ready to cook, but I like to leave it on the counter or a tray for 30 minutes or so to dry out a bit. (The drier the pasta, the more time it'll take to cook and the more time you'll have to do any last-minute prep.) You can store it in a plastic storage container (in a loose tangle for tagliatelle and pappardelle, in a stack with a piece of parchment paper between each layer for cannelloni) in the refrigerator for up to 2 days.

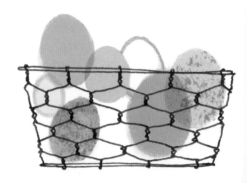

TAGLIATELLE WITH ASPARAGUS AND PARMESAN FONDUTA

This entire dish is right out of Rose and Ruthie's River Café playbook, with just a few tweaks of my own. They taught me how to make fonduta, a silky sauce rich with crème fraîche and egg yolks. It takes less time and just a bit more effort than tomato sauce, and turns a plate of pasta into an elegant and impressive meal. Get yourself some asparagus spears that are as thick as your pointer finger—not those thin or sprouty ones—and you'll enjoy the juicy slivers in each bite.

Bring a large pot of water to a boil.

Meanwhile, bring an inch or two of water to a boil in a small pot. Whisk together the egg yolks, crème fraîche, Parmesan, and garlic in a large heatproof bowl that will fit snugly in the pot without making contact with the boiling water.

Set the bowl in the small pot and whisk the egg mixture constantly, occasionally scraping the sides and removing the bowl from the pot every couple of minutes as you whisk to keep the cooking nice and slow (don't let it bubble). The mixture will look thick and clumpy for a few seconds, then become liquidy, and then, once the cheese has melted, silky smooth. Cook just until the liquidy sauce has thickened slightly (it should thinly coat the back of a spoon), 6 to 8 minutes. Set the bowl aside in a warm place.

Salt the large pot of boiling water generously until it tastes slightly less salty than the sea. If you're confident that the pasta and asparagus will finish cooking at the same time, add them both to the water. If you're a worrywart, cook the asparagus first, scoop it into a colander to drain, then cook the pasta. Cook the asparagus until it is juicy with a slight bite, 3 to 4 minutes; and cook the pasta until it is fully cooked, 3 to 4 minutes.

Drain the pasta and asparagus well in a colander, then pop them back into the now-empty pot. Pour in most of the fonduta and toss gently but well. Season to taste with salt and more fonduta, if you'd like. Transfer to bowls, top with a little more Parmesan, and eat straightaway.

serves 4 as a main

2 large egg yolks

1½ cups crème fraîche

5 ounces Parmesan cheese, finely grated, plus a bit more for finishing

1 medium garlic clove, finely grated on a rasp-style grater

Kosher salt

1 pound asparagus, woody bottoms snapped off, stalks cut on the diagonal into long ½-inch-thick pieces, tips left whole

½ recipe Fresh Egg Pasta (page 127), cut into tagliatelle

vegetable pastas, polenta, pastries, and friends **133**

PAPPARDELLE WITH CHANTERELLE MUSHROOMS

Like ramps and truffles, chanterelles—or *girolles* to those of us raised across the pond—resist cultivation. They're one of the few remaining foods that only grow wild. And so they're available for a short time and you must pay dearly for them. Dearly but gladly, if you ask me. Of the two main varieties, golden and yellow foot, I much prefer the denser golden chanterelles that pop up in markets in late summer to early fall to the skinny, rather watery yellow foots that come around in winter. When cooking golden chanterelles, there's no better strategy than keeping things simple. At all costs, you want to avoid masking their earthy, fruity (reminiscent of apricots!) flavor by meddling too much. So I apply one of my favorite trios of ingredients—garlic, butter, parsley—and serve the chanterelles with eggy homemade pasta, all of which keep the spotlight on those wild, wonderful mushrooms.

Bring a large pot of water to a boil and salt the water generously until it tastes slightly less salty than the sea. Leave small chanterelles (those with caps smaller than a nickel) whole. Cut the others lengthwise into ¼-inch-thick slices so that you get some that show off the mushroom's pretty silhouette.

Heat the oil in a large, heavy skillet over medium-high heat until it smokes lightly. Add the garlic and cook, stirring frequently, until the garlic is golden brown and smells toasty, 30 seconds to 1 minute. Reduce the heat to medium-low, add the butter, and let it melt and froth. Add the mushrooms and 1 teaspoon of Maldon salt, have a stir, then cover the skillet. Cook, stirring occasionally, just until the mushrooms are tender, 2 to 3 minutes. Add ½ cup of fresh water and turn off heat.

Cook the pasta in the salted boiling water until it's a minute or so away from al dente, about 3 minutes, then drain the pasta well.

serves 4 to 6 as a main

Kosher salt

1 pound fresh golden chanterelles, cleaned (see "Cleaning Wild Mushrooms," opposite)

2 tablespoons extra-virgin olive oil

2 medium garlic cloves, thinly sliced

6 tablespoons unsalted butter, cut into several pieces

Maldon or another flaky sea salt

Fresh Egg Pasta (page 127), cut into pappardelle

2 teaspoons lemon juice, plus more to taste

A small handful of delicate flat-leaf parsley sprigs, roughly chopped

A handful of finely grated Parmesan cheese

Turn the heat under the skillet to high, and let the liquid come to a vigorous simmer. Add the pasta, lemon juice, and parsley, toss well, and cook, tossing occasionally, until the pasta is al dente and the liquid has evaporated but the pasta still looks glossy, 1 to 2 minutes. Season to taste with salt and just enough lemon juice to add brightness, not acidity. Divide among plates, sprinkle on the Parmesan, and serve straightaway.

CLEANING WILD MUSHROOMS

To clean the mushrooms, cut away any brown bits from the bottom of the stems. Fill a big bowl with water, add the mushrooms, and use your hands to gently submerge them in the water and agitate them a bit, rubbing them gently if the visible dirt is particularly stubborn. Do not keep the mushrooms in the water for more than 20 seconds or so. Transfer to a kitchen towel to drain and pat dry.

SWISS CHARD CANNELLONI

All you need for a winter dinner party are these trays of cannelloni filled with velvety, lemony chard. Add a big old salad of bitter greens and everyone's happy. Instead of the typical lake of béchamel sauce that often drowns cannelloni, I prefer using a lighter hand with a more delicate mixture of cream, milk, and lemon zest. Otherwise, the dish would be too heavy and less about the fresh pasta and the chard. As it all bakes, the little pools of cream thicken and go golden at the edges, and the tops of the pasta tubes get a bit bubbly and crispy.

Ready a large bowl of icy water. Grab a few clean kitchen towels, get them damp, and lay out one on a work surface.

Bring a large pot of water to a boil and add enough kosher salt so it tastes lightly salty. Cook the pasta in batches, 6 or so sheets at a time, in the boiling water for 1 minute, and transfer the sheets as they're done to the icy water, using your hands to help them lay flat (not folded or doubled over) in the water.

Lay as many rectangles of pasta on the towel as will fit in one layer, cover them with another towel, and repeat until they're all laid out and covered.

Combine the chard in a bowl with the ricotta, ¼ cup of the Parmesan, the egg, 2 teaspoons of the Maldon salt, and pepper to taste and stir really well.

Lightly coat the bottoms and sides of 2 large, heavy enameled baking dishes with olive oil (about 1 tablespoon per dish).

Grab a rectangle of pasta, lay it on your work surface, and spread about 1½ tablespoons of the chard mixture along one of the short sides, leaving a bit of space at the edges. Starting from the side with the filling, roll the rectangle over the filling into a neat cylinder, transfer it to one of the baking dishes, and repeat with the rest of the filling and pasta. It's fine if not all of the cylinders line up the same

serves 8 to 10 as a main

SPECIAL EQUIPMENT
2 large, heavy enameled baking dishes (each about 10 x 14 inches)

Kosher salt

Fresh Egg Pasta (page 127), prepped for cannelloni

Swiss Chard (Leaves and Stems) with Marjoram (page 75), at room temperature

1 pound ricotta

2 ounces Parmesan cheese, finely grated

1 large egg, lightly beaten

3 teaspoons Maldon or another flaky sea salt

Freshly ground black pepper

6 tablespoons extra-virgin olive oil

4 medium garlic cloves, thinly sliced

2 cups heavy cream

1 cup whole milk

½ teaspoon packed finely grated lemon zest

A five-finger pinch of basil leaves

A five-finger pinch of tender fennel fronds

vegetable pastas, polenta, pastries, and friends   **137**

way in the pan. Drizzle about 1 tablespoon of olive oil over each baking dish.

Position a rack in the center of the oven and preheat to 450°F.

Heat the remaining 2 tablespoons of oil in a large skillet over high heat until it shimmers. Add the garlic and cook, stirring frequently, until the garlic is light golden brown and smells toasty, 30 seconds to 1 minute. Add the cream, milk, lemon zest, and remaining 1 teaspoon of Maldon salt to the skillet. Let the mixture come to a full boil, then pour it evenly over the cannelloni. I like to leave the parts of the cannelloni at the edges of the dish unsauced, so they get a bit crispy later during baking. Sprinkle ½ cup or so of the Parmesan over the cannelloni.

Bake the cannelloni until it has brown patches on top and the sauce at the edge of the dishes has gone golden brown, about 20 minutes.

Roughly chop the basil and fennel fronds and sprinkle them over the cannelloni along with the remaining Parmesan. Serve straightaway.

LUMACONI STUFFED WITH SUMMER VEGETABLES

Lumaconi is dried pasta in the shape of a big snail shell that just begs to be stuffed. I often fantasize about what I can stuff them with. The first time I ate lumaconi, they were filled with sausage. The first time I made them, it was springtime, and I filled the shells with Jerusalem artichokes, peas, and tomatoes. This recipe is for summer, a sort of succotash in pasta form. Into each shell, you spoon a simple stew of tomatoes, corn, zucchini, and green beans, which gets some meaty complexity from slow-cooked red onion and garlic. Pour on a little cream and into the oven goes the pasta to get a bit toasty and crispy.

Bring a large pot of water to a boil. Fill a big bowl with icy water. Add the tomatoes to the boiling water, wait 15 seconds (or 30 seconds if you've got especially firm tomatoes), then use a spider to gently transfer them to the icy water. Be sure to keep the water in the pot at a boil.

Peel the tomatoes, discarding the skins, and set them aside.

Refill the big bowl with cold water. Generously salt the boiling water until it tastes a little less salty than the sea. Add the pasta and cook according to instructions on the package until al dente, about 9 minutes. Drain well, put the pasta in the bowl of cold water, and let the pasta sit just until it's fully cool. Transfer the pasta opening side down to a plate lined with paper towels to drain.

Cut the corn kernels from the ears, then use the back of your knife to scrape each cob to get at any bits of kernel left behind. Combine the kernels and scrapings in a bowl. Cut the cobs into a few pieces and pop them into a medium pot along with the cream and ½ teaspoon of the Maldon salt. Bring the cream to a boil over high heat, then remove the pot from the heat.

Rinse and wipe the large pot. Pour in the oil and set the pot over medium-high heat until the oil shimmers. Add the onion and 1 teaspoon of the Maldon salt and cook, stirring occasionally, until wilted,

1¾ pounds cherry tomatoes (about 2 pints), each pricked with the tip of a sharp knife

Kosher salt

9 ounces dried lumaconi pasta (about 30) or jumbo shell pasta

2 large ears corn, shucked

2½ cups heavy cream

2½ teaspoons Maldon or another flaky sea salt

¼ cup extra-virgin olive oil

1 medium-large red onion (about ¾ pound), halved lengthwise and thinly sliced

3 medium garlic cloves, thinly sliced

A small handful of basil leaves, roughly chopped at the last minute

3 dried pequín chiles, crumbled, or pinches of red pepper flakes

½ pound zucchini, topped, tailed, and cut into ½-inch irregularly shaped pieces (about 2 cups)

5 ounces green beans, topped, tailed, and cut into 1-inch pieces (a generous cup)

A handful of finely grated Parmesan cheese

about 5 minutes. Push the onion to the side, add the garlic to the slick of oil, and cook until it's toasty and turns a light golden color, 1 to 2 minutes. Give it all a good stir, cover, reduce the heat to medium-low, and cook until the onions are very soft, about 10 minutes. Stir in half the basil and cook, uncovered, stirring occasionally, until the onions are lightly browned, about 8 minutes more.

Add the tomatoes and the remaining 1 teaspoon of the Maldon salt to the pot and cook, stirring and mashing the tomatoes, until they've released their liquid and are almost completely broken down, about 12 minutes. Add the corn, increase the heat to bring the mixture to a strong simmer, and cook until the kernels are tender but still have a pop, about 5 minutes. Add the chiles, zucchini, green beans, and the remaining basil and cook at a strong simmer, stirring, until the zucchini and green beans are tender with a slight snap, 5 to 8 minutes. Remove the vegetables from the heat.

Position a rack in the center of the oven and preheat to 400°F.

Grab a heavy enameled baking dish large enough to fit the lumaconi in a single layer with a little room to spare. Fill each noodle with about 2 tablespoons of the vegetable mixture and add them opening side up to the baking dish.

Discard the corncobs, then pour the cream evenly over the stuffed lumaconi. Bake until the cream has thickened and turned light golden at the edges of the dish, about 20 minutes. Sprinkle on the Parmesan, turn on the broiler, and cook just until the cheese has turned light golden brown in spots, 3 to 5 minutes more. Let the dish cool just slightly and serve.

KALE POLENTA

In the U.S., polenta is typically served as a side dish. But in Italy, it is often the main attraction—a real showstopper. I've been seated at a table with friends when the cook arrived from the kitchen with the pot of polenta. Instead of ladling the polenta onto our empty plates, as I first expected, the cook poured the polenta from the pot straight onto a wooden board in the center of the table. Steamy and inviting, it crept outward like hot lava.

My Kale Polenta is a showstopper in its own right: its striking green color is beautiful and unexpected. It's so stunning you can skip the board and just haul the pot to the table. The healthy dose of kale puree that colors the cornmeal adds lots of flavor, too. You taste the sweetness of the corn polenta first, then a hint of garlic, and finally that green minerality of kale at the end.

Combine 7 cups of water and the salt in a medium pot and bring the water to a boil over high heat. Gradually add the polenta, whisking as you pour. Keep whisking until the polenta starts to thicken and looks like it's one with the water, about 2 minutes. Turn the heat to low (the polenta should steam and tremble, but only rarely erupt with bubbles) and cook, stirring every now and again, until the polenta is tender but still slightly coarse in texture, about 45 minutes.

Stir in the olive oil, kale puree, and most of the Parmesan and keep cooking, stirring occasionally, for a few minutes more. Take the pot off the heat and fold in 2 tablespoons of the mascarpone (it's nice to run into a little pocket of mascarpone, so don't stir too much). Top with the remaining mascarpone and Parmesan, and as much black pepper as you'd like.

serves 6 to 8 as a side

1 tablespoon plus 1 teaspoon Maldon or another flaky sea salt

2 cups coarse stone-ground polenta, such as Anson Mills brand

¼ cup extra-virgin olive oil

½ cup Kale Puree (page 235)

2 ounces Parmesan cheese, finely grated

3 tablespoons mascarpone

Coarsely ground black pepper

SWEET-CORN POLENTA

When you can get your mitts on high-quality stone-ground stuff, polenta becomes more than just a vehicle for butter and Parmesan. Great polenta has character—a pleasantly coarse texture and the unmistakable flavor of corn. I like to add summer's finest fresh corn, with the soft crunch of its kernels and its unparalleled sweetness, to underscore the polenta's flavor and contrast its texture.

Cut the corn kernels from the cobs, then use the back of the knife to scrape each cob to get at any bits of kernel left behind. Combine the kernels and scrapings in a bowl, and reserve the cobs.

Cut the cobs crosswise into a few pieces, combine them with 7 cups of water in a medium pot, and cover the pot. Bring the water to a boil over high heat, then uncover the pot and remove and discard the cobs.

Stir in the salt, then gradually add the polenta, whisking as you pour. Keep whisking until the polenta starts to thicken and looks like it's one with the water, about 2 minutes. Turn the heat to low (the polenta should steam and tremble, but only rarely erupt with bubbles) and cook, stirring every now and again, for 20 minutes. Stir in the corn kernels and scrapings and continue to cook the polenta until it's tender but still slightly coarse in texture, about 25 minutes more.

Take the pot off the heat, stir in the butter and most of the Parmesan, then season with salt to taste. Sprinkle on the remaining Parmesan and as much black pepper as you'd like.

serves 6 to 8 as a side

4 medium ears corn, shucked

1 tablespoon plus 1 teaspoon Maldon or another flaky sea salt

2 cups coarse stone-ground polenta, such as Anson Mills brand

3 tablespoons unsalted butter

2 ounces Parmesan cheese, finely grated

Coarsely ground black pepper

BUTTERNUT SQUASH POLENTA

There are earthy, creamy chunks of winter squash lurking in this pot of polenta. I stir in the squash roughly, so it's not entirely incorporated and some stays in larger pieces. That way, each bite is different. And I love getting a sneaky hit of heat from the chile. You can roast the squash as the polenta bubbles, which means this dish takes only slightly more effort and almost no extra time than plain old polenta.

Position a rack in the center of the oven and preheat to 450°F.

Combine 7 cups of water and 1 tablespoon plus 1 teaspoon of the salt in a medium pot and bring the water to a boil over high heat. Gradually add the polenta, whisking as you pour. Keep whisking until the polenta starts to thicken and looks like it's one with the water, about 2 minutes. Turn down the heat to low (the polenta should steam and tremble, but only rarely erupt with bubbles) and cook, stirring every now and again, until the polenta is tender but still slightly coarse in texture, about 45 minutes. Cover and keep the polenta warm over very low heat.

Meanwhile, toss the squash with ¼ cup of the oil, the garlic, the remaining 2 teaspoons of salt, and the chiles in a heavy enameled baking dish large enough to fit the squash in a single layer with a little room to spare. Pour ½ cup of water into the pan (around but not over the squash), cover the pan tightly with foil, and bake until the squash is fork-tender, 30 to 40 minutes. Remove the foil and bake until the squash is very tender but not mushy and the bottoms have browned a bit, about 15 minutes more.

Add the squash, including any bits stuck to the pan, to the polenta and have at it with a whisk, stirring and smashing so some of the squash is incorporated into the polenta and some remains in chunks.

Stir in the remaining 2 tablespoons of oil, the butter, and most of the Parmesan. Take the pot off the heat and fold in 2 tablespoons of the mascarpone (it's nice to run into a little pocket of mascarpone, so don't stir too much). Top with the remaining mascarpone and Parmesan, and as much black pepper as you'd like.

serves 6 to 8 as a side

1 tablespoon plus 3 teaspoons Maldon or another flaky sea salt

2 cups coarse stone-ground polenta, such as Anson Mills brand

2 pounds butternut squash, peeled, seeded, and cut into irregular 2-inch chunks

¼ cup plus 2 tablespoons extra-virgin olive oil

2 medium garlic cloves, finely chopped and smooshed to a paste

3 dried pequín chiles, crumbled, or pinches of red pepper flakes

2 tablespoons unsalted butter

2 ounces Parmesan cheese, finely grated

3 tablespoons mascarpone

Coarsely ground black pepper

FOCACCIA

I know good focaccia when I put a knife through it—when the blade cracks through the crust with a crunch, and I can't help but smile. That crunch and an airy crumb tell me right away that I'm not about to eat one of those dense, dry versions that have threatened to tarnish the bread's reputation. Although the best breads often come from great bakeries, where the people running the place have spent years perfecting their craft, focaccia is one of those relatively simple breads that home cooks can manage. This recipe is based on Nancy Silverton's, because she's just brilliant. The neat part about making focaccia yourself is not just that you get to eat it when it's good and fresh, but that you get to experience all the little joyous moments along the way, like when your *biga* (the starter) develops happy bubbles and when the dough becomes elastic and smooth as a baby's bum. Focaccia makes a delicious vehicle for vegetables, too. I provide two options of toppings—one with butternut squash and another with thinly sliced potatoes—but I hope you'll have fun coming up with your own.

make the biga

About twenty-four hours before you plan to bake the focaccia: Combine the tepid water and yeast in a small bowl and stir with a wooden spoon until the yeast has dissolved, 30 seconds or so. Put the bread flour in a medium bowl, pour in the yeast mixture, and stir until the flour is incorporated and the ingredients are well combined.

Cover the bowl tightly with plastic wrap and leave in a warm place until the mixture looks bubbly and has thickened (when you tip the bowl it should just barely creep forward), 18 to 24 hours.

make the dough

A few hours before you plan to bake the focaccia, combine the yeast, bread flour, 1 tablespoon of the oil, 1¼ cups of water, and all of the biga in the bowl of a stand mixer fitted with a dough hook. Mix on low speed until you have a uniform dough (about 1 minute), then increase the speed to medium, slowly sprinkle in the salt, and mix, stopping to

makes two 8-inch rounds

SPECIAL EQUIPMENT
A stand mixer with dough hook attachment and two 8-inch round cake pans (2 inches deep)

FOR THE BIGA
Scant ½ cup tepid water

Scant ⅛ teaspoon packed cake yeast or scant ¹⁄₁₆ teaspoon active dry yeast (not instant or rapid-rise)

4 ounces (1 cup minus 1 tablespoon) bread flour

FOR THE DOUGH
34 grams cake yeast, crumbled, or 17 grams (1 tablespoon plus 2 teaspoons) active dry yeast (not instant or rapid-rise)

17 ounces bread flour (about 3¾ cups), plus a little extra as needed

1 tablespoon extra-virgin olive oil, plus a glug for coating the bowl

1 tablespoon kosher salt

scrape down the sides of the bowl if need be, just until the dough is smooth and elastic and it begins to pull away from and slap against the bowl of the mixer, 6 to 8 minutes. If the dough is too moist, it won't pull away from the bowl, so if need be, gradually add a little more flour. If the dough is too dry, it won't be smooth, so if need be, gradually add a little more water.

Turn the dough onto a lightly floured surface and use your hands to make sure the ball of dough is nice and round.

Add a glug of olive oil to a bowl large enough to hold at least twice the amount of dough, then wipe the bowl with a paper towel to coat it with a thin layer of the oil. Add the dough, cover the bowl tightly with plastic wrap, and put it in a warm place until it has doubled in size, 1 to 1½ hours.

top and bake the focaccia
While the dough is doubling, make the topping of choice.

Pour ¼ cup of the oil into two 8-inch round cake pans and tilt them so the oil covers the surfaces.

FOR TOPPING AND BAKING
Butternut, Sage, and Chiles (page 151) or Potatoes, Red Onion, and Thyme (page 152)

¼ cup extra-virgin olive oil, plus a glug for baking

vegetable pastas, polenta, pastries, and friends **149**

Turn the dough onto a lightly floured surface and cut it in half. (I like to be precise and weigh the dough. You'll have about 2 pounds, and each half should weigh about a pound.) Add a half to each cake pan and use your fingers to gently pull the edges of the dough toward the sides of each pan. Cover the pans tightly with plastic wrap and put them in a warm place until the dough relaxes and has puffed up a little, about 25 minutes.

Spread the topping evenly onto the dough, leaving about a ½-inch border. Press down gently so the topping sinks in slightly, and gently push the edges so they more or less reach the sides of the cake pan. Cover with plastic wrap again and let it puff up a little more, 15 to 30 minutes.

Position a rack in the center of the oven and preheat to 450°F. Drizzle on a little more olive oil (about 1 tablespoon), put the focaccia on the center rack and bake, rotating the pans once, until the crust and undersides (use a spatula to have a peek) are light golden brown, about 25 minutes.

Transfer the pans to a rack to cool slightly, then slice however you wish and eat the focaccia warm or at room temperature.

BUTTERNUT, SAGE, AND CHILES

enough for two 8-inch focaccia

3 tablespoons extra-virgin olive oil, plus a healthy drizzle for finishing

1½ pounds butternut squash, peeled, seeded, and cut into ½-inch cubes (about 3½ cups)

6 medium garlic cloves, thinly sliced

5 or so dried pequín chiles, crumbled, or pinches of red pepper flakes

A small handful of sage leaves, torn if large

1½ teaspoons plus a healthy pinch Maldon or another flaky sea salt

½ ounce aged pecorino cheese (preferably pecorino ginepro), finely grated on a rasp-style grater

While the focaccia dough is doubling, make the topping: Heat the oil in a medium skillet over medium-high heat until it smokes lightly. Add the squash (it's OK if it's not in one layer) and cook, stirring and tossing occasionally, just until the edges begin to brown, 5 to 7 minutes. The squash cubes will still be slightly crunchy in the middle.

Push the squash to one side of the skillet. Add the garlic to the empty side and sprinkle the chiles over the squash. Cook the garlic, stirring until it's golden brown at the edges, about 1 minute, then mix everything together. Cook for a minute more, add the sage and 1½ teaspoons of Maldon salt, and remove the pan from the heat. Stir well and let the mixture cool.

Top and bake the focaccia as directed (page 149). After removing the focaccia from the oven, sprinkle them with a healthy pinch of Maldon salt, add a healthy drizzle of olive oil (2 to 3 tablespoons) to the topping and crust, and sprinkle on the pecorino.

POTATOES, RED ONION, AND THYME

enough for two 8-inch focaccia

5 ounces fingerling, baby Yukon Gold, or small purple potatoes, unpeeled

3 tablespoons extra-virgin olive oil

1 small red onion (a generous ¼ pound), halved lengthwise and thinly sliced

A five-finger pinch of thyme leaves, coarsely chopped

2 medium garlic cloves, finely grated on a rasp-style grater

1½ teaspoons Maldon or another flaky sea salt

2 tablespoons packed pitted, roughly chopped Niçoise or Taggiasca olives

A few splashes of red wine vinegar

While the focaccia dough is doubling, make the topping: Use a vegetable peeler to shave the potatoes lengthwise into irregular thin slices. As you work, immediately put the slices in a medium mixing bowl with 2 tablespoons of the oil (to prevent browning) and toss well. Add the onion, thyme, and garlic and toss well. Top and bake the focaccia as directed (page 149), sprinkling on the salt just before you pop the pans in the oven.

Meanwhile, stir together the olives, the remaining 1 tablespoon of oil, and the vinegar. After removing the focaccia from the oven, spoon the olive mixture here and there on top of the focaccia and serve.

MUSHROOM PIES WITH SWISS CHARD

There's a football chant used to taunt players who look less than fit on the field. "Who ate all the pies?" your team's fans all ask at once, before everyone answers, "You fat bastard, you fat bastard!" Of course, the fans aren't talking about blueberry or cherry pie; the British use of the word refers first and foremost to all manner of savory filled pastries (though a few pies, like shepherd's, have no pastry at all). There's kidney pie, beef and Stilton pie, and pork pie, the latter so famous someone named a hat after it. In Cornwall, you'll find stargazy pie, which features sardine-like fish with their heads poking out of the top crust as if they were gazing at the stars. There are too many pies to list them all. The point is that they're so common and so beloved that to fans, pies are the inevitable culprit behind lethargic footballers.

I too remember feeling a bit sluggish after taking down a chicken and mushroom pie at the pub or chippy. While you wouldn't want a pie to be light—then it'd no longer be a pie, would it?—I do think of this version as a little more elegant than my girlhood favorites. I leave out the meat altogether, opting instead for mushrooms (sturdy, common ones for bulk and texture, and wild ones for flavor) with a touch of cream for richness. I add chard, because I like the way its lemony quality brightens the pie. Each pie is an ample dinner with a simple salad.

make the dough

Combine the flour, sugar, and salt in a large mixing bowl and stir very well. Add the butter to the flour mixture and toss to coat with flour. Then work swiftly (the last thing you want is for the butter to melt) to break up and smoosh the butter lumps with your fingertips just until none are much bigger than peas.

Pour in the buttermilk and water, stir well with a fork, then use your hands to swiftly scrunch and pack (don't knead) the mixture just until it comes together into a blob. If there's lots of loose flour, gradually add more water, then scrunch and pack again. Cut the dough in half, wrap each half in plastic wrap, and refrigerate the dough for at least 1 hour or up to 12 hours.

makes four 5-inch pies

SPECIAL EQUIPMENT

4 nonstick mini (5-inch) pie pans

FOR THE DOUGH

2½ cups all-purpose flour

1 tablespoon granulated sugar

1 teaspoon kosher salt

½ pound (2 sticks) very cold unsalted butter, cut into ½-inch pieces just before using

½ cup cold well-shaken buttermilk

1 tablespoon cold water, or more if necessary

FOR THE FILLING

4 tablespoons (½ stick) unsalted butter

1 medium Spanish onion (about ½ pound), thinly sliced

2 medium garlic cloves, thinly sliced

1 tablespoon thyme leaves, roughly chopped

2 teaspoons Maldon or another flaky sea salt

(continued on next page)

make the filling

Melt the butter in a medium pot over medium heat. Add the onion, garlic, thyme, and 1 teaspoon of the Maldon salt and cook, stirring occasionally, until the onion is very soft with just a kiss of brown, about 20 minutes. Use a slotted spoon to transfer the mixture to a bowl, leaving the butter behind.

Increase the heat to medium-high, add the chard stems to the pot, and cook, stirring and scraping the pot, until they're lightly browned at the edges, about 5 minutes. Add the mushrooms to the pot and cook, stirring almost constantly for a minute. Add the onion mixture and the remaining 1 teaspoon of salt. Cook, stirring and scraping often, until the mushrooms are just cooked through and the chard stems are tender with a slight crunch, about 5 minutes. Pour in the cream, let it come to a boil, then remove the pot from the heat. Let the mixture cool completely. You can make this up to a day in advance.

Pour just enough water into a large skillet with a lid to barely cover its surface. Bring the water to a boil, add the chard leaves, and pop on the lid. Cook, stirring once, until the leaves are fully wilted and tender, about 3 minutes. Drain the chard, let it cool to the touch, and squeeze out as much liquid as you can. Give the leaves a rough chop and stir them into the mushroom mixture.

make and bake the pies

Position a rack in the center of the oven and preheat to 375°F.

Take one of the dough halves from the fridge and cut it into 4 equal pieces. Lightly flour your work surface. Working with one piece at a time (and keeping the others, covered, in the fridge), roll the dough into a rough 7-inch round that's about ⅛ inch thick. Lay it in one of the pie pans, gently pressing it against the bottom and up the sides so it fits securely. Use a knife to trim off the overhang and then put the pie shell in the fridge while you roll out the three remaining pieces. Chill the shells in the fridge for 30 minutes or so.

1 pound green Swiss chard, stems trimmed and cut on the diagonal into ½-inch-wide slices, leaves torn in half

6 ounces mixed wild mushrooms, separated or cut into about 1½ x ½-inch pieces (about 3 cups)

¼ pound portobello caps, peeled and cut into irregular pieces about as large as the other mushrooms (1 generous cup)

1 cup heavy cream

4 teaspoons crème fraîche

1 large egg yolk

1 tablespoon whole milk

Cut four 6-inch squares of parchment paper. Crumple each square into a ball, wet the ball under running water, squeeze out all the water, then flatten out the squares again. (This makes them more malleable.) Line each pie shell with a piece of parchment paper and fill it with uncooked rice or dried beans, using your fingers to make sure the rice or beans go all the way to the edges. Put the pie pans on a baking sheet and bake, rotating the baking sheet once, just until the rim of the dough no longer looks raw, about 15 minutes.

Take the pans out of the oven, wait 5 minutes or so, then carefully remove the parchment and rice or beans. (You can save the rice or beans to use the next time you bake.) Divide the filling among the 4 crusts and add 1 teaspoon of crème fraîche to the center of each pie.

Whisk together the egg yolk and milk in a small bowl. Brush the rim of the crusts with some of the egg mixture. Take the remaining dough from the fridge and cut it into 4 equal pieces. Working with one piece at a time (and that's keeping the remaining pieces covered in the fridge), roll into a 7-inch round about ⅛ inch thick, lay the rounds over each pie and press them lightly against the edge of the crust so they adhere. Trim off any overhang with a knife and crimp the edges of the pie. Brush the tops with the egg mixture, return the pies to the baking sheet, and bake them, rotating the sheet occasionally, until the tops are golden brown, about 35 minutes.

Carefully invert each dish; the pie should slip right out. If not, use a knife to make sure the edges have separated from the pan. Serve them tops up on plates and eat straightaway.

vegetable pastas, polenta, pastries, and friends **155**

BUTTERNUT SQUASH-COCONUT TART

My first Thanksgiving, when I had my first taste of pumpkin pie, was fairly typical—you know, just me sitting at a long table with Mario Batali and his family. I was fresh off the boat from London, just after I became the chef of The Spotted Pig. I didn't know anyone in New York and Mario was kind enough to invite me to share his holiday meal. I remember being quite nervous, because I'd made a pumpkin caponata (a sort of sweet-sour savory relish typically made from eggplant) and I hoped Mario would like it. Someone had brought a pumpkin pie, which I had assumed, being from the land of meat pies, would be a savory dish as well. I was surprised when it came out for dessert. Yet I adored it. Pumpkin—as well as winter squashes like butternut—is one of those vegetables that's as at home during dinner as it is after. So long as there's not too much spice getting in the way of the earthy, melony squash flavor, I'm a big fan. This is my favorite version, with a sneaky bit of coconut milk providing richness and a compelling something special that your mates will love, even if they can't quite identify the source. A good dollop of whipped cream and a sprinkle of toasted coconut flakes make a nice topping.

make the tart shell

Sift the flour into the food processor, then add the powdered sugar, butter, and salt. Pulse the mixture until it looks like fine breadcrumbs. Add the egg yolks and pulse until a crumbly dough forms. Scrape the dough out onto a work surface and lightly knead just until smooth. Form the dough into a ball, wrap it in plastic wrap, and refrigerate it for at least 1 hour or up to 2 days.

Position a rack in the center of the oven and preheat to 350°F.

Cut the chilled dough into 2 or 3 large pieces and grate it through the large holes of a box grater. Use your fingers to press the dough onto the bottom and up the sides of the pie dish to create an even layer that's about ¼ inch thick on the sides and ⅜ inch thick on the bottom. (If you're using the 9-inch pie dish, you'll have enough dough and fill-

makes one
9½-inch tart

SPECIAL EQUIPMENT
A heavy 10-inch fluted pie dish (about 3 inches deep) or a heavy 9-inch pie dish (about 2 inches deep)

FOR THE TART SHELL
2¼ cups all-purpose flour

¾ cup powdered sugar

12 tablespoons (1½ sticks) cold unsalted butter, cut into ¼-inch pieces

¼ teaspoon plus ⅛ teaspoon kosher salt

3 large egg yolks, lightly beaten

FOR THE FILLING
8 cups cubed (about 1 inch), peeled butternut squash (from a 3-pound squash)

1½ cups well-stirred canned unsweetened coconut milk

1 cup superfine sugar

⅛ teaspoon ground cinnamon

5 large eggs plus 1 egg yolk

ing left over to make a mini pie, a special treat for the cook.) Work swiftly—you don't want the dough to warm up too much. Gently prick the bottom here and there with a fork, which will prevent it from puffing up as it bakes, then pop the dish into the freezer for 15 minutes.

Cut out a 12-inch round of parchment paper and line the dough with it. Fill the tart shell with uncooked rice or dried beans, using your fingers to make sure the rice or beans go all the way to the edge. Put the tart shell on a baking sheet and bake just until the rim begins to turn light golden brown, about 15 minutes. Carefully remove the parchment paper and rice or beans. Let the shell cool while you make the filling. Keep the oven on.

make the filling

Put the squash in a heavy enameled baking dish in a single layer, cover the dish tightly with foil, and bake, stirring once and re-covering tightly with foil, until the squash is very soft, about 55 minutes. Leave the oven on.

Transfer the squash to a blender. Add the coconut milk and puree until very smooth. With the blender running on low, add the sugar, cinnamon, and one at a time, the whole eggs and the egg yolk. Keep the blender running just until the eggs are fully incorporated into the mixture.

Put the tart shell on a baking sheet. Pour just enough of the squash mixture into the tart shell to come up to about ¼ inch from the rim, reserving the rest for the mini pie. Bake, rotating the pan once, until the crust is golden brown and the filling has just set, 45 minutes to 1 hour. After about 30 minutes, take a peek at the exposed crust. If it already looks light golden brown, carefully cover the exposed crust with foil for the remainder of the baking time.

Remove the pan from the oven and let the tart cool to room temperature before slicing. It keeps covered in the fridge for up to a day or two.

BROCCOLI RAAB MORNING BUNS

If you've never heard of a morning bun, your first order of business should be popping over to San Francisco and heading to Tartine Bakery. Behind the glass of the display case, you'll spot spiral-shaped little pillows baked with orange-cinnamon sugar, the center of each one rising up like a hill. That is, if you haven't arrived too late. They're magic, really—buttery layers of dough that are somehow both rich and delicate, crackly on the outsides and soft in the middle. Whenever I cook them, they get me thinking. As a cook obsessed with Italian food, the orange element brings to mind rosemary (the two often join forces in Sicily), which brings to mind all sorts of savory, Italianesque options, like this version laced with pesto made from pleasantly bitter raab and musty, sharp aged provolone.

make the yeast dough

Combine 1 cup of the warm milk and the yeast in a small mixing bowl and stir with a wooden spoon until the yeast has mostly dissolved. Let the mixture sit until the surface bubbles, about 5 minutes.

In the bowl of a stand mixer fitted with the dough hook, stir together the flour, sugar, and salt. Add the yeast-milk mixture, then swish the remaining ¼ cup of warm milk in the small bowl to get at any yeast left behind and pour it into the bowl of the stand mixer. Mix on low speed for 2 minutes. If there's still loose flour visible after the dough forms, gradually add up to 2 tablespoons more warm milk until all of the flour is incorporated.

Increase the speed to medium-low (if your mixer is struggling a bit, take out the dough, cut it in half, and work one piece at a time) until the dough is smooth and slightly tacky, 3 to 4 minutes.

Add a glug of oil to a bowl large enough to hold at least twice the amount of dough, then wipe the bowl with a paper towel to coat it with a thin layer of the oil. Add the dough, cover the bowl tightly with plastic wrap, and leave it at room temperature until it has increased in size 1½ to 2 times, 30 minutes to 1 hour. Put it in the fridge overnight.

makes 12 buns

SPECIAL EQUIPMENT

A stand mixer with dough hook and paddle attachments, two 6-cup jumbo muffin tins, and a rolling pin

FOR THE YEAST DOUGH

1¼ cups whole milk, gently heated just until warm to the touch, plus 2 tablespoons as needed

1 ounce cake yeast, crumbled, or 1 tablespoon plus 1 teaspoon active dry yeast (not instant or rapid-rise)

18 ounces (about 3¾ cups) all-purpose flour

2 tablespoons granulated sugar

2 teaspoons kosher salt

A glug of neutral oil, such as canola

FOR THE BUTTER BLOB

1 pound (4 sticks) cold unsalted European-style butter, such as Plugrá, cut into about ½-inch slices

2 tablespoons all-purpose flour

make the butter blob

Wash the bowl of the stand mixer and fit the mixer with the paddle attachment. Combine the butter and flour in the bowl. Mix at low speed for 10 seconds or so, then at medium speed until the butter and flour are well combined and there are no lumps but not so long that the butter is no longer cold, about 1 minute. Transfer the blob to a clean surface and work swiftly to shape it into a 7 x 6-inch rectangle. Wrap it in plastic and pop it in the fridge until it's well chilled, at least 8 hours or overnight.

make the morning bun dough

Take the butter blob from the fridge and let it sit at room temperature for a minute or two just to take the chill off. Do not let it get warm. Put the yeast dough on a clean, lightly floured surface and use a heavy rolling pin to roll it into a rough 16 x 7½-inch rectangle. Position the dough so a long side faces you. Put the butter blob in the center of the dough so its slightly shorter side faces you. Fold one of the dough's short sides over the butter so it just covers half of the butter. Fold the opposite side so it covers the other half of the butter. Gently pinch together the dough edges at the center to seal in the butter.

Roll from short end to short end, flipping over the dough once and dusting it and the work surface with flour so it won't stick to the pin or surface, until you have an even rectangle that's about 22 x 9 inches. (To achieve the 9-inch width, you might have to rotate the dough 90 degrees and roll briefly.)

Fold the dough into thirds as though it were a letter, gently wiping away the excess flour on the top and bottom of the dough as you do: Start by folding one of the short sides to create an approximately 15 x 9-inch rectangle, then fold the other short side to create an approximately 7½ x 9-inch rectangle. Wrap the dough in plastic wrap and refrigerate for 1 hour. You're going to repeat this process three more times, so each time, scribble down a number to keep track of how many you've completed.

FOR THE PESTO FILLING

3½ cups lightly packed roughly chopped broccoli raab (stalks that are ¼ inch or thinner, leaves, and florets)

3 medium garlic cloves, roughly chopped

4½ ounces aged provolone, roughly chopped

3 tablespoons extra-virgin olive oil

1 tablespoon drained, stemmed, finely chopped oil-packed Calabrian chiles (about 3) or 1 teaspoon crumbled dried pequín chiles

1 tablespoon Maldon or another flaky sea salt

Wait a few minutes until the chill comes off the dough so it's easier to roll, but don't let it get warm. Position the dough so that the rounded side faces your left. Then gently roll the dough into an even rectangle that's about 22 x 9 inches. For the second time, fold the dough into thirds as though it were a letter. Wrap the dough in plastic wrap and refrigerate for 1 hour. Repeat the process—rolling, folding, and refrigerating—twice more.

meanwhile, make the pesto filling

Working in batches if necessary, combine the broccoli raab and garlic in a food processor, and pulse, stirring occasionally, until the raab is finely chopped and there are no large pieces of garlic. Transfer the mixture to a mixing bowl. Add the provolone to the processor and pulse until it's in small chunks, then transfer it to the bowl. Add the oil, chiles, and salt and stir well.

bake the buns

Roll the dough out to an even 18 x 12-inch rectangle.

Spread the pesto evenly onto the dough, leaving a ½-inch border on all sides. Use your hands to roll up the dough to form a tight 18-inch-long log. Run wet fingers along the seam, then turn the log seam side down and press down gently so the seam adheres.

Cut the log crosswise into twelve 1½-inch-thick pieces. Put the slices into the cups of the jumbo muffin tins and lightly press down so they touch the bottoms of the cups. Cover them loosely with plastic wrap (or even better, use an overturned clean plastic tub to avoid the risk of the plastic wrap sticking after the dough rises) and keep them in a warm place until the dough rises a bit above the rim, about 1 hour.

Meanwhile, position a rack in the center of the oven and preheat to 475°F. Bake the buns on the rack (if both muffin tins can't fit on the center rack, bake in two batches) until they're croissant-golden-brown and crispy, 12 to 15 minutes. Carefully pry them out of the muffin tins and let them cool slightly on a wire rack.

simple things
broccoli raab

Sweetness is easy to love. Too easy. I think that's why I love bitter vegetables so much: because loving them requires a little effort. Take broccoli raab. When I was a girl, I would never have chosen the slightly acrid, minerally green vegetable over peas, let alone a Cadbury Cream Egg or a Curly Wurly. And even though our taste buds change as we get older, I didn't wake up one day and suddenly crave broccoli raab. The appreciation came slowly. I had to eat it again and again before I turned the corner. That's very adult, isn't it? To realize that the people and things and pleasures that are worth one's while take work.

So I say, seek out broccoli raab that has a real bite. Have a nibble of a raw leaf, and make sure its bitterness is intense, that it makes you perk up as it catches the back of your tongue. At home, I'll often do little more than sauté broccoli raab with garlic, salt, and chile, which provide balance that lets you enjoy the bitterness. Trim off any brown or woody bottoms, then get a few good glugs of olive oil hot in a heavy skillet. Add a few thinly sliced garlic cloves and move them around, watching as they get golden brown and toasty. Crumble in a bit of chile, then add your raab, making sure not to crowd the pan, or else it'll steam. Cook, tossing occasionally, until the raab stems are tender with a slight snap. Sometimes I like when the raab has just a kiss of brown. Sometimes I increase the heat so the raab goes all wilty and crispy. Sprinkle on some flaky sea salt and have another toss. With vegetables this bitter, life sure is sweet.

a little beast
goes a long way

SWEET POTATOES WITH BONE MARROW, CHILE, AND MAPLE SYRUP

My mate Fergus Henderson has long celebrated the glories of marrow at his restaurants, where he roasts veal shank bones until the marrow inside is wiggly, perfect for scooping out and spreading onto bread. I also use marrow as if it were beefy butter, though in this dish I go a different route: the bones roast along *with* the sweet potatoes. The marrow melts into the pan, soaking into the potatoes, helping them go brown and crispy.

Position a rack in the center of the oven and preheat to 450°F.

Put the potato rounds in a medium pot, pour in just enough water to cover them by about ½ inch, and add the kosher salt. Bring the water to a boil over high heat, lower the heat to maintain a strong simmer, and cook the potatoes just until they're fully tender (a knife will meet the slightest resistance in the center of each slice), 15 to 20 minutes. Drain them well and let them sit uncovered in the colander for about 15 minutes.

Put the rounds flat on your work surface. Gently but firmly squeeze the sides of each round so the flesh at the edges smooshes and cracks a bit. This will help the marrow penetrate the flesh of the potatoes. Arrange the rounds in a heavy enameled baking dish (large enough to fit the potatoes and marrow bones in a single layer with a little space between them) and stand the marrow bones here and there between them. Drizzle the oil evenly over the potatoes and bones, sprinkle with the chiles, and add a healthy sprinkle of Maldon salt over the top of each round and bone.

Pop the dish into the oven and cook, rotating the pan once or twice, until the undersides of the potatoes are deep brown, crispy, and a bit sticky, 30 to 40 minutes. Flip the potatoes (if the oven is properly hot, they should release easily from the dish), but not the bones, and cook until the second sides are deep brown and crispy as well, 20 to 30 minutes more. Use a spatula to transfer the potatoes to a plate, spoon on a little of the fat from the baking dish, drizzle with the maple syrup, and sprinkle with Maldon salt to taste.

serves 4 as a side

2 pounds sweet potatoes, unpeeled, topped, tailed, and cut crosswise into 1½-inch-thick rounds

3 tablespoons kosher salt

1 pound center-cut veal marrow bones, cut by your butcher into 1½- to 2-inch lengths

¼ cup extra-virgin olive oil

4 dried pequín chiles, crumbled, or pinches of red pepper flakes

Maldon or another flaky sea salt

3 tablespoons pure maple syrup

BROCCOLI WITH BACON

On its surface, there's not much to this dish, really. Yet as with so much of the food I love, it's the small details in the cooking that result in something special. In this case, the pot is the key. If you use one that has nice high sides (anywhere from 6 to 10 inches high) and that's wide enough to hold the broccoli snugly in one layer, the broccoli will fry in the porky fat but also steam a bit, so that by the time it's lightly browned it'll also be perfectly cooked—right at that sweet spot between crunchy and soft. Before I serve the dish, I like piling the onions and bacon on the broccoli so everyone can have a go at it with their fingers.

Heat the oil in a medium pot over high heat until it shimmers. Add the bacon and cook, stirring and scraping frequently, just until the edges of the bacon are browned and crispy, 2 to 3 minutes. Use a slotted spoon to transfer the bacon to a bowl, leaving the fat behind.

Add the broccoli to the bacon fat, stir it well, and top it with the onion. Cook, without stirring, until the broccoli begins to brown a bit, about 3 minutes, then stir and cook, stirring frequently, until the onion looks wilted and golden at the edges, about 3 minutes more.

Reduce the heat to medium-low and add the chiles and the reserved bacon. Cook, stirring occasionally, for about 5 minutes. Sprinkle on the salt and cook about 5 minutes more, until the broccoli stems are fully tender with a slight bite.

Transfer it all to a plate and squeeze on just enough lemon juice to provide brightness, not acidity. Serve straightaway.

serves 4 to 6 as a side

¼ cup extra-virgin olive oil

¼ pound thinly sliced bacon, cut into ¾-inch pieces

1 medium broccoli head, cut into 2 x 2-inch florets, stems trimmed, peeled, and cut into 1-inch lengths (about 6 cups)

1 medium Spanish onion (about ½ pound), halved and thinly sliced

2 dried pequín chiles, crumbled, or pinches of red pepper flakes

1 teaspoon Maldon or another flaky sea salt

½ lemon

BRAISED COLLARDS WITH BACON, VINEGAR, AND CHILES

The first time I confronted collard greens—at Martha Lou's, a wonderful Charleston restaurant that specializes in soul food—I was a bit timid. I had never had collards in England. From what I'd heard, collards were strongly and unpleasantly flavored—quite cabbagy and rough around the edges, at the opposite end of the spectrum from lemony, feminine chard. One bite of Martha Lou's collards, however, and I found that, like most notorious foods, when done right—as they were—they were delicious. Cooked with some smoky pork until they were very, very tender, these collards were right up my alley, especially since I come from England, the land of long-cooked vegetables.

My version begins with braised bacon. The braising liquid becomes a flavorful broth in which the collards cook, along with plenty of vinegar and chiles. Once the collards are ready, not only will they be supremely silky, though not as soft as the true Southern rendition, they will have absorbed the flavors of the pork and vinegar, which round off their rough edges.

Combine the bacon, garlic, onion, and thyme in a large pot with 8 cups of water. Bring the water to a simmer over high heat. Cover, lower the heat to maintain a steady simmer, and cook until the bacon is very tender (you should be able to insert a sharp knife by exerting only a little pressure) but not falling apart, about 1 hour. Uncover and discard the thyme stems.

Add the vinegar, tomatoes, and chiles to the pot and stir. Increase the heat to high and bring the liquid to a boil. Let the liquid boil, stirring occasionally, until it has reduced by about half, about 25 minutes. It's fine if the bacon falls into large chunks, but try not to break it into stringy bits as you stir.

Meanwhile, cut the collards crosswise into 1-inch-wide strips. Measure out 24 lightly packed cups; reserve any extra for another purpose.

serves 6 to 8 as a side

½-pound piece smoked slab bacon, halved

6 medium garlic cloves, halved lengthwise

1 small red onion (about ¼ pound), peeled and halved

2 healthy thyme sprigs

½ cup apple cider vinegar

⅓ cup drained, trimmed, and coarsely chopped canned whole tomatoes (see page 16)

2 to 4 dried ají dulce peppers or 4 to 6 dried pequín chiles, crumbled

3 large bunches collard greens, stems thicker than ¼ inch removed

Maldon or another flaky sea salt

Add the sliced collards to the pot, pressing them down so they all fit. Cover the pot, wait until the collards wilt slightly, 2 minutes or so, then stir well. Cover the pot again, lower the heat to maintain a steady simmer, and cook, using tongs to toss and stir occasionally, until the collard leaves are very tender and the stems have just a slight bite, about 30 minutes.

Uncover, increase the heat a bit, and cook at a strong simmer, stirring now and then, so some of the liquid cooks off, about 10 minutes. Have a taste. You might need to add some salt if your bacon wasn't salty to start with. Serve straightaway.

STEAMED EGGPLANT WITH GROUND PORK AND THAI BASIL

This dish is definitely a Brummie girl's take on the classic Sichuan-style eggplant—if you are looking for "authenticity," fair warning. When I cook at home, I adapt dishes to fit my fussy ways. I latch on to the parts I like—Asian cooks often use meat almost like a seasoning, which I think is just grand—and put aside the ones I don't. Very rarely, for example, do I add sugar to savory things. I happily eat Thai salads, Chinese stir-fries, and other dishes that rely on a tablespoon or two for balance or contrast. But in my kitchen, I'd rather pull natural sweetness from garlic, onions, and the like. I like the result a lot, even though some might moan that it's not the real thing. It's a good job, then, that I don't run a Chinese restaurant. Serve this with steamy white rice and you've got a meal for four.

Put a steamer insert (or a colander, so long as the pot's lid can still close) in a large pot. Add enough water to reach about ½ inch in depth, cover the pot, and bring to a boil over high heat. Season the eggplant lightly with salt, add to the steamer, cover, and steam until the pieces are fully tender and creamy, 12 to 15 minutes.

Meanwhile, heat the oil in a medium pot over high heat until it begins to smoke. Add the onion and garlic and cook, stirring constantly, until they begin to brown and smell sweet, about 2 minutes. Add the pork and cook, stirring, scraping the pot, and breaking up the meat, until it's golden brown in spots and just cooked through, 2 to 3 minutes. Add the stock, fish sauce, and soy sauce and let the liquid come to a simmer. Lower the heat to maintain a gentle simmer and cook, occasionally stirring and scraping the bottom of the pot, for about 5 minutes more, so the flavors come together.

Add the eggplant and basil to the pot and stir very gently. Raise the heat to medium-high. Cook, uncovered, at a vigorous simmer, for a few minutes, then add the lime juice and continue cooking, occasionally shaking the pan but not stirring, until the liquid has reduced to a slightly viscous consistency, 12 to 15 minutes. Serve while it's still steamy.

serves 4 to 6 as a side

2 medium eggplants (about 1¾ pounds), topped, tailed, quartered lengthwise, and cut crosswise into irregular 1½-inch-thick pieces

Maldon or another flaky sea salt

1 tablespoon neutral oil, such as safflower or grapeseed

½ cup finely chopped red onion (from about 1 small)

3 medium garlic cloves, finely chopped

½ pound ground pork

1 cup Simple Chicken Stock (page 245)

1 tablespoon plus 1 teaspoon fish sauce

1 tablespoon soy sauce

A five-finger pinch of Thai basil (tender stems and leaves), roughly chopped

1 tablespoon lime juice

a little beast goes a long way

CABBAGE-STUFFED CABBAGE

Inexpensive and plentiful, lowly cabbage is rarely the star of a dish. Even when the vegetable headlines, as in stuffed cabbage, it typically takes a backseat to the meaty filling. Not so here, since I stuff cabbage with, well, more cabbage. I quite like the way the dish showcases two different textures of the same vegetable—the sturdiness of the boiled leaves and the silkiness of the braised cabbage inside them. Like most versions of stuffed cabbage, this one's hearty thanks to the meatiness of the vegetable, but it remains light and bright thanks to a finishing dose of lemon and Parmesan.

Combine the oil and butter in a wide heavy pot and set it over medium heat. When the butter melts, add the bacon and carrots first and then the onion on top. Sprinkle on 1½ teaspoons of the Maldon salt and pop on the lid. Cook, without stirring, until the bacon looks a bit translucent, 5 to 7 minutes. Have a stir and keep cooking, covered, stirring now and again and lowering the heat if necessary, until the onions are very soft but not colored, about 15 minutes.

Meanwhile, remove and discard the outermost leaves of the cabbage. Carefully remove 12 large leaves and set aside. Halve, core, and thinly slice the remaining cabbage until you get 10 cups. Reserve any remaining cabbage for another use.

Add the stock to the pot and bring it to a boil over high heat. Add the sliced cabbage and 1 teaspoon of the Maldon salt. Cover the pot, reduce the heat to medium, and cook at a simmer, stirring now and then, until the cabbage is fully tender but not mushy, about 7 minutes. Take the pot off the heat.

Bring a medium pot of water to a boil over high heat and season it with kosher salt until it tastes nice and salty. Boil the 12 reserved cabbage leaves in two batches until they're soft enough that you can fold them without breaking them, 3 to 4 minutes per batch. Drain them well, let them cool a bit, and pat them dry.

serves 4 as a main

¼ cup extra-virgin olive oil, plus a healthy drizzle for finishing

4 tablespoons (½ stick) unsalted butter, plus more for the baking dish

5 ounces smoked bacon (slab or thick slices), cut into ¼-inch cubes (about 1 cup)

¼ pound carrots, peeled, topped, tailed, and cut into ¼-inch cubes

1 medium-large Spanish onion (about ¾ pound), halved lengthwise and thinly sliced

2½ teaspoons plus a generous sprinkle Maldon or another flaky sea salt

2 Savoy cabbage heads (about 1½ pounds each)

1 cup Simple Chicken Stock (page 245)

Kosher salt

1 ounce Parmesan cheese, finely grated on a rasp-style grater

Freshly ground black pepper

½ lemon

Generously butter a large, heavy enameled baking dish (large enough to hold the cabbage rolls snugly in a single layer). Lay the boiled leaves on a work surface, concave sides up. (If they have very thick stems, flip the leaves over and use a knife to shave off a bit of stem, then flip them back over.) Give the cabbage-bacon mixture a good stir, then use a slotted spoon to divide it evenly among the leaves, leaving a ½-inch border. Reserve the liquid for basting. Sprinkle a generous pinch of Parmesan onto each dollop of filling. Roll each leaf over the filling to form a fairly snug cylinder with open ends, then transfer it seam side down to the baking dish.

Turn on the broiler. Pop the baking dish in the oven about 4 inches from the heat source and cook, basting occasionally with some of the reserved cooking liquid, until the cabbage rolls are very lightly browned on top and hot through, 3 to 5 minutes. Sprinkle the remaining Parmesan over the top, then add a generous sprinkle of Maldon salt, a few turns of black pepper, and a drizzle of olive oil. Squeeze on just enough lemon so it all tastes bright, but not acidic. Eat straightaway.

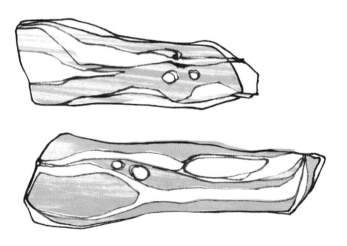

ROASTED MUSHROOMS WITH PANCETTA, PINE NUT BREADCRUMBS, AND GOAT CHEESE

The porky sweetness of pancetta, the crunch of breadcrumbs, and the tang of goat cheese make this collection of roasted mushrooms moreish—each bite is a bit different and tempts you to take yet another. Taking a minute to carefully arrange the ingredients on a baking sheet just before they go into the oven also makes the dish special. I like to position the mushrooms just so, so the larger ones get good and tender and the smaller ones get a bit crispy. I tuck the thyme between the mushrooms so it doesn't burn. I wrap the pancetta in and around the mushrooms, because, well, it just feels right. My favorite part comes at the end when everything is all roasty and the juices have pooled in the pan. I tip the juices into a small pot, reduce them so their flavor concentrates, then spoon them back on.

Position a rack in the center of the oven and preheat to 400°F. Line a large baking sheet with parchment paper.

Halve the portobello caps (I like to cut on a diagonal instead of vertically here) and arrange the halves gill side down on the baking sheet so the cut sides face each other and the corner of one of the halves is propped up on the corner of the other. Leave about an inch of space between each pair. Divide the oyster mushrooms more or less evenly among the portobello pairs, arranging them here and there around and on top of the portobellos. Lay two pancetta slices on each pair. I like to curl them around the oyster mushrooms and tuck an end under the portobellos. Tuck 2 of the thyme sprigs between each pair of portobello halves. Arrange any larger maitake clusters around the portobellos and put small ones on top.

Divide the garlic slices and the butter (one piece per portobello pair) in little blobs here and there on top of the mushrooms. Over each por-

serves 6 as a side

6 medium portobello mushrooms, stems removed, caps peeled

½ pound oyster mushrooms, thick stems trimmed, mushrooms separated

12 thin, long slices pancetta

12 thyme sprigs

½ pound maitake mushrooms, thick stems trimmed, separated into smaller clusters

3 medium garlic cloves, very thinly sliced

4 tablespoons (½ stick) unsalted butter, cut into 6 more or less even pieces

1¾ teaspoons Maldon or another flaky sea salt

6 tablespoons extra-virgin olive oil, plus a healthy drizzle for finishing

3 ounces slightly stale rustic bread, such as filone, crust discarded, pulled into about 1-inch pieces (about 1 cup)

(continued on next page)

tion, sprinkle about ¼ teaspoon of the Maldon salt, drizzle about 1½ teaspoons of the olive oil, and pour 2 tablespoons of water.

Roast in the oven until the portobellos are fully tender (a sharp knife inserted in the thickest part should meet very little resistance), the maitake mushrooms have browned a bit, and the pancetta is slightly brown at the edges but still a bit floppy, 30 to 40 minutes. After 15 minutes and occasionally thereafter, take the tray from the oven, tip it so the juices pool, and use a spoon to baste each portion. (If there is barely any juice, pour ¼ cup or so of water onto the tray.)

Meanwhile, put the bread in a food processor and pulse to form very coarse crumbs (a mixture of pebbly bits and chunks, ½ inch at the largest). Put the crumbs in a medium skillet along with the pine nuts, toss well, and add the remaining 3 tablespoons of olive oil. Set the pan over high heat, wait for the oil to sizzle, and cook, tossing and stirring constantly, until the bread is crunchy and the pine nuts are peanut-butter brown, about 3 minutes. Drain the crumbs and pine nuts in a sieve, give them a good shake, and transfer to paper towels to fully drain. Sprinkle on a little salt.

When the mushrooms are ready, carefully tip the pan and let the liquid run off into a small saucepan. Bring it to a boil over high heat and cook until it reduces a bit and tastes flavorful and a bit salty, about 5 minutes.

Use a spatula to transfer each portion to plates. Sprinkle on more salt to taste, drizzle on a little olive oil, then add a squeeze of lemon for brightness, not acidity, and a spoonful or two of the reduced mushroom liquid. Sprinkle on the breadcrumb mixture, put large pieces of the cheese here and there, and add the arugula. Dig in straightaway.

Heaping ¼ cup pine nuts

½ lemon

About 3 ounces Humboldt Fog or other young goat cheese

A handful of delicate, peppery arugula

chilly weather treats

WINTER-SQUASH PANCAKES WITH SQUASH SYRUP AND PECAN BUTTER

Winter squash is a perfect breakfast component, as breakfast is much the same as squash: both can go in either a savory or sweet direction. Some mornings I crave smooshed roasted squash on toast with floppy bacon and fried eggs. On others I look to this dish, in which the squash provides earthy sweetness to the batter and the maple syrup as well. I have a bit of fun serving the pancakes in a big old stack, tucking a couple slivers of pecan butter between each cake, topping the stack with a good knob of it, too, then pouring on the syrup at the table so it dribbles dramatically down the sides.

makes sixteen
4- to 5-inch pancakes

4 heaping cups peeled, seeded, and cubed (about 1½ inch) butternut squash

1 cup all-purpose flour

¾ cup stone-ground polenta

1½ teaspoons baking soda

1½ teaspoons baking powder

1 tablespoon plus 2 teaspoons granulated sugar

¼ teaspoon kosher salt

1 cup well-shaken buttermilk

1 cup whole milk

1 large egg

¾ cup pure maple syrup

A few glugs of extra-virgin olive oil

About 6 tablespoons room-temperaure Spiced Pecan Butter (page 183) or plain salted butter

Preheat the oven to 400°F. Put the squash in a heavy enameled baking dish large enough to fit the squash in more or less one layer. Pour in ¼ cup of water, cover the dish tightly with foil, and bake, stirring once, until the squash is very soft but not falling apart, about 45 minutes. If there's still water in the dish, remove the foil and bake just until the water's gone, about 5 minutes more. Let the squash cool a bit and puree it in a food processor until very smooth.

Lower the oven heat to 200°F.

Combine the flour, polenta, baking soda, baking powder, sugar, and salt in a large mixing bowl and whisk well. Add the buttermilk, milk, egg, and ¾ cup of the squash puree and whisk until the mixture is smooth.

Stir together the maple syrup and ½ cup of the remaining squash puree in a small pot, reserving the remaining squash for another purpose. Gently heat the mixture until it's warm and keep it warm over very low heat.

Preheat a heavy griddle over medium heat until it's good and hot, then reduce the heat to medium-low. Use a paper towel to rub a thin layer of oil onto the griddle. Cook the pancakes in batches (use about ¼ cup batter per pancake), flipping them once with a sturdy spatula, until they're golden brown on both sides and fully cooked, 6 to 8 minutes. Transfer the pancakes to a plate and keep them in the warm oven. Between each batch, rub a little more oil on the griddle.

Serve in stacks with a pat of pecan butter tucked between each pancake and a couple on top, drizzle on the syrup, and serve straightaway.

SPICED PECAN BUTTER

makes 1 generous cup

¼ cup pecan halves

1 medium guajillo chile (about 5 x 1 inch), slit open, seeded, and deveined

½ teaspoon crumbled dried pequín chiles or red pepper flakes

2 sticks (½ pound) unsalted butter, at room temperature

2 tablespoons pure maple syrup

½ teaspoon kosher salt

Position a rack in the center of the oven and preheat to 350°F. Spread the pecans in a single layer on a small baking sheet and bake, tossing occasionally, until they're aromatic but not colored, 3 to 5 minutes. Transfer them to a cutting board, let them cool, and roughly chop until no bits are larger than ¼ inch.

Preheat a skillet over medium heat, add the guajillo, and toast, flipping once and occasionally pressing down on the chile, until aromatic, 1 to 2 minutes. Let it cool, combine in a spice grinder with the pequín chiles, and buzz to a fine powder.

Combine the pecans, chile powder, butter, maple syrup, and salt in a bowl and mix and mash until the ingredients are very well distributed. Spread the butter in a rough log shape on a piece of plastic wrap, roll the wrap tightly around the butter, and twist the edges to seal.

Use it straightaway, refrigerate for up to 5 days, or cut into portions and freeze in airtight packages for up to 1 month.

ROASTED TREVISO WITH BREADCRUMBS AND GORGONZOLA

Treviso, a type of radicchio with longer leaves, is one of my pet vegetables. I love how the burgundy leaves contrast with the pure white stems. I love how astringent Treviso is, how after you handle it, its bitterness stays on your fingertips. But not everyone enjoys this quality and for those people, this dish is the answer. As the Treviso roasts, its bitterness mellows, the hearts get creamy, and the leaves go slightly crispy at the edges. And the sweetness of the pine-nut breadcrumbs, the acidity of the vinaigrette, and the saltiness of the cheese all balance the whisper of bitterness remaining.

Position a rack in the center of the oven and preheat to 400°F.

Put the pine nuts in a mortar and pound until they're crushed to the texture of couscous. Pop them in a bowl. Combine the garlic and 1 teaspoon of the salt in the mortar and pound to a coarse paste, then add the marjoram and pound to a fine paste. Add the pine nuts, breadcrumbs, ¼ cup of the olive oil, and 1 tablespoon of water to the mortar and stir well.

Slice into the root ends of the Treviso, about 1½ inches into the head. You're not trying to split the halves; this is just to help the heat penetrate this particularly dense part. Arrange the halves cut sides up in a heavy enameled baking dish just big enough to fit them in a single layer.

Working with one Treviso half at a time and separating the leaves carefully with your hands so they stay attached, use a spoon to tuck and spread a heaping tablespoon or so of the breadcrumb mixture onto the bottom leaf, another between the leaves near the middle, and another between the leaves near but not quite at the top of the halves. Sprinkle the remaining breadcrumb mixture on the top of each Treviso half.

Drizzle the root ends with a little olive oil and sprinkle with salt.

serves 6 as a side

¼ cup pine nuts

1 medium garlic clove, peeled

1¼ teaspoons plus a generous pinch Maldon or another flaky sea salt

A five-finger pinch of marjoram leaves

½ cup slightly coarse dried breadcrumbs

¼ cup plus 3 tablespoons extra-virgin olive oil, plus more for drizzling

3 medium heads Treviso (about 1 pound), root ends trimmed of brown bits but left intact, outermost leaves removed, halved lengthwise

2 teaspoons red wine vinegar

6 ounces mountain Gorgonzola (also called piccante), cut into 12 rustic-looking chunks

3 ounces arugula

Cover the dish tightly with foil and bake until the root ends are fully soft and creamy, about 35 minutes. Remove the foil, increase the temperature to 500°F, and keep roasting, rotating the pan once, until the Treviso leaves are shriveled and a bit crispy, and the visible breadcrumbs are golden brown, 10 to 15 minutes more.

Meanwhile, in a small bowl, whisk together the vinegar, the remaining 3 tablespoons of the oil, and ¼ teaspoon of the Maldon salt until the mixture looks creamy. Drizzle half of the vinaigrette over the heads while they're still hot.

Let the Treviso cool to warm or room temperature. Divide the Treviso among 6 plates. Put 2 chunks of Gorgonzola next to each head. Right before you're ready to serve, gently toss the arugula with the remaining dressing in a bowl and pile some next to each head.

DOSA WITH CURRIED CAULIFLOWER AND YOGURT

I don't think I'd ever had a dosa, a type of crepe made from a fermented lentil and rice batter, before coming to New York. My hometown of Birmingham has a big Pakistani and Indian population, but not so many people from South India, where the dosa comes from. Vegetarianism goes hand in hand with religion there, so creative cooks have come up with an entire universe of incredibly tasty, sophisticated, and satisfying meatless food. Even though the dosa comes from a place with a hot climate, I find it perfect for eating in chilly weather.

The first time I had a dosa, I ordered a couple of types at a restaurant, not quite knowing what to expect. The waiter arrived bearing this massive golden, crispy cylinder, which was almost twice as long as the plate it came on. Another version was smaller, softer, and spongier, but just as delicious. Its fermented tang reminded me of Parmesan cheese. I ate quickly, because they were so good and because I could barely wait to have a go at making them myself. It turns out that once you get the hang of it, they're pretty easy to replicate at home (well, not so much those massive ones). Of course, if you're like me, you'll be shit-scared at mucking up the first few. To help, this recipe makes plenty of batter. And even your unsuccessful practice dosa will be tasty to nibble on.

make the dosa batter

Combine the rice and the two types of dal in a large mixing bowl and add 10 cups of water. Stir well and cover the bowl with cheesecloth or a lid left slightly ajar. Leave the bowl at room temperature (and away from any cool drafts) to ferment until the mixture smells slightly sour and looks a bit frothy, about 24 hours. If you like your dosa a little more sour, which I do, let it ferment for another 12 to 24 hours.

Drain the rice mixture, reserving 4 cups of the liquid. Blend the rice mixture with 3 cups of the reserved liquid until completely smooth,

serves 4 to 6 as a main

FOR THE DOSA BATTER

2 cups basmati rice

1 cup white urad dal (see note, page 189)

¼ cup chana dal (see note, page 189)

1 teaspoon Maldon salt

FOR COOKING AND FILLING THE DOSAS

Several teaspoons extra-virgin olive oil

Maldon or another flaky sea salt

Curried Cauliflower with Peas (page 190), warm

Generous ¼ cup Greek yogurt

A small handful of delicate cilantro sprigs, roughly chopped

gradually adding up to another 1 cup of the liquid if necessary to achieve a texture like that of heavy cream. When you're ready to make the dosa, stir in the salt until it has dissolved.

cook and fill the dosa

Heat a large nonstick skillet over medium heat until it's good and hot. Before you cook the first dosa, add about ½ teaspoon of oil to the pan and swirl the pan to coat the bottom as best you can. Between dosa, wipe the pan clean.

Stir the batter well before making each dosa. Spoon about ¼ cup of the batter into the center of the pan and using an implement with a flat bottom, such as a metal measuring cup, spread the batter into a very thin round about 8 inches in diameter. Start in the center and spread the batter outward using a circular motion. You need a really light touch to get the batter nice and thin without creating any big holes (tiny holes form naturally and that's a good thing). You'll get

better with each one you make—and you have plenty of batter, so don't fret if you bungle the first few. I often do.

After spreading the batter, add a very light drizzle of oil and a light sprinkle of salt to the surface of the dosa. Let the dosa cook, without messing with it, until the edges begin to brown and lift from the pan and the underside is a light golden color, 1½ to 2 minutes. Use a spatula to gently lift an edge, then transfer the dosa to a plate—it should come away from the pan easily and cleanly. Spoon ½ to ¾ cup of the curried cauliflower to one side of the dosa. Add a dollop of yogurt and a generous pinch of the chopped cilantro. Fold the dosa over the filling to make a semicircle and serve straightaway while you get to work on the remaining dosa.

Note: Urad dal are small black beans that resemble split lentils, and come in several forms: whole, split, and split and husked. For this recipe, buy the latter form, which is off-white in color. Chana dal is a small sibling of the chickpea that has been split and husked. Both are available at Indian markets and online.

CURRIED CAULIFLOWER with PEAS

Although I originally designed this as filling for my take on the South Indian crepe called dosa (page 187), I'd eat it on its own any day with some basmati rice to make it a meal. I'm by no means an expert on Indian cooking. I just love it. I fell for the food growing up in Birmingham, where good curry shops sometimes seem to outnumber good pubs. I idolize Madhur Jaffrey, who did for Indian cooking in America what Marcella Hazan did for Italian cooking. Who knows, she might taste this and take a dim view. But I think it's quite tasty.

Heat the oil in a medium pot over medium-high heat until it smokes lightly. Add the onion, stir well, and cook, stirring occasionally, until wilted and just beginning to color, about 3 minutes. Add the garlic and chile and cook, stirring, until the onion has browned in spots, 3 to 5 minutes more.

Add the cauliflower and cilantro stems to the pot and cook, stirring occasionally, just until the cauliflower has picked up some of the brown color from the onion, about 2 minutes. Add the tomatoes, garam masala, and salt and cook, stirring frequently, until the tomato is thick and jammy, about 5 minutes.

Stir in the peas and ½ cup of water, scraping the sides and bottom of the pot to get at that nice browned stuff. Pop a lid on the pot, reduce the heat to maintain a steady simmer, and cook, stirring occasionally, until the cauliflower is fully tender but not mushy and the liquid has thickened a bit, about 20 minutes. (You might have to remove the lid for the last 5 minutes to help the liquid evaporate.) Stir in the yogurt, turn off the heat, and let the curry sit covered for a few minutes so the flavors can meld. Serve straightaway.

The curry keeps for a day or two in the fridge. Add a splash of water and gently warm it before serving.

serves 4 as a side

3 tablespoons extra-virgin olive oil

1 medium red onion (about ½ pound), halved lengthwise and thinly sliced

3 medium garlic cloves, thinly sliced

1 red Thai or another small, very spicy fresh chile, thinly sliced (including seeds)

1 small head cauliflower, trimmed and cut into 2 x 2-inch florets (about 3 cups)

2 generous tablespoons very thinly sliced cilantro stems

⅔ cup drained, trimmed, and finely chopped canned whole tomatoes (see page 16)

1 tablespoon garam masala (preferably homemade, page 240)

1 tablespoon Maldon or another flaky sea salt

10-ounce package frozen baby peas

1 heaping tablespoon Greek yogurt

CURRIED PARSNIP SOUP

I remember making my first curries and fretting that they were quite bland. Now I know it was because I was being French with the shallots, rather than taking them quite dark, as an Indian cook would, to add rich complexity. The coconut milk and garam masala are, of course, key players in this soup, but the unsung heroes of the dish are actually the apples. Their acidity is a perfect counterpoint to the sweetness of the parsnips, and it lends a hint of brightness to the deep flavor of the shallots.

Heat the oil in a medium pot over medium-high heat until it smokes lightly. Add the shallots, stir well, and cook, stirring and scraping the pan frequently so nothing burns, until they're very soft, sweet, and deep golden brown, about 10 minutes. Add the garlic and cook, stirring frequently, until it's light golden brown, 2 to 3 minutes.

Add the parsnips, apples, garam masala, salt, and 5 cups of water and stir well. Turn the heat to high, bring the water to a boil, then lower the heat to maintain a gentle simmer. Cook for 20 minutes or so, then add the coconut milk and cream. Bring the liquid back to a gentle simmer and cook until the parsnips and apples are fully soft, about 45 minutes more.

Pour the soup into a large mixing bowl. Working in batches, blend the soup (be careful when blending hot liquids) until very smooth and silky, adding each batch back to the pot. Season to taste with salt and serve it straightaway or keep it in the fridge for up to 3 days.

serves 6 to 8

¼ cup plus 2 tablespoons extra-virgin olive oil

½ pound shallots (about 3 large), halved lengthwise and thinly sliced

4 medium garlic cloves, very thinly sliced

2¼ pounds parsnips, peeled, topped, tailed, and cut into 1-inch pieces

1¼ pounds sweet-tart apples, such as Empire (about 3), peeled and cut into 1-inch pieces

2 teaspoons garam masala (preferably homemade, page 240)

1 tablespoon plus 1 teaspoon Maldon or another flaky sea salt

1 cup well-stirred canned coconut milk

½ cup heavy cream

SLOW-ROASTED LEEKS WITH WALNUT BREADCRUMBS

Leeks are wonderful when prepared in the French bistro style: simply poached, then bathed in vinaigrette. I tweak the classic, slow-roasting the poached leeks to accentuate their sweetness and succulence, and adding contrast with walnut breadcrumbs that get crunchy as the leeks get softer. While leeks vinaigrette is typically served cold or at room temperature, I like to dress the leeks straight from the oven and eat the dish while it's good and hot. For this dish, choose leeks that have a good long portion (about 9 inches) of white and light green.

Position a rack in the center of the oven and preheat to 400°F.

Cut off the dark green parts from the leeks. Remove and discard the outermost layer (you might have to remove the second layer as well if it feels woody). Trim the roots and any brown bits but keep the root end intact. Cut each leek crosswise to separate the white part from the light green part. Make a lengthwise cut through half of each piece, leaving the rest of the half intact (this will help with swishing out the grit). Soak the leeks in a big bowl of cold water for a few minutes, gently separating the layers with your fingers to expose any gritty bits and swishing a bit, then drain them.

Meanwhile, combine the halved garlic head, lemon zest, thyme, bay leaves, 2 teaspoons of the salt, and 6 cups of water in a large, wide pot. Bring to a boil over high heat and boil for 5 minutes or so, just to infuse the liquid with flavor.

Add the white leek halves to the water, wait a minute, then add the light green halves. Let the water come back to a boil, then lower the heat to maintain a steady simmer. Cook, carefully turning the leeks occasionally, until they're just tender (a sharp knife inserted in a leek should meet with a little resistance), 8 to 12 minutes. Using a spider or slotted spoon, carefully transfer the leeks to a kitchen towel to

serves 4 to 6 as a side

5 large leeks (about 3½ pounds), each about 1½ inches wide

1 large head garlic, halved crosswise, plus 1 medium clove, roughly chopped

4 strips (3 x ¾ inch) lemon zest

4 small thyme sprigs

2 fresh bay leaves

2½ teaspoons Maldon or another flaky sea salt

½ cup walnut halves

A five-finger pinch of delicate flat-leaf parsley sprigs, roughly chopped

¼ cup coarse dried breadcrumbs

½ cup extra-virgin olive oil

2 tablespoons roasted walnut oil

1 tablespoon plus 1 teaspoon red wine vinegar

2 teaspoons Dijon mustard

drain and let them sit until cool to the touch. Pat them dry. Reserve a generous tablespoon of the cooking liquid.

Combine the garlic clove and remaining ½ teaspoon salt in a mortar and pound to a fine paste. Add the walnuts and gently pound them so they break into ½- to ¼-inch pieces. Scoop out a good tablespoon or two of the walnuts and set aside. Add the parsley to the garlic-walnut mixture in the mortar and pound to a coarse paste. Stir in the reserved walnuts, the breadcrumbs, and ¼ cup of the olive oil.

Heat the remaining ¼ cup of olive oil in a heavy enameled baking dish (large enough to hold the leeks side by side with a little room to spare) over medium-high heat until it shimmers. Add the leeks and cook, carefully flipping them over once, until they're lightly browned on both sides, about 3 minutes. Line them up prettily in the dish so they're touching, then scatter the breadcrumb mixture on top.

Pop the dish in the oven and bake, rotating the pan once, until the crumbs are crispy, the nuts are toasty, and the leeks are fully tender, 20 to 30 minutes.

Meanwhile, whisk together the walnut oil, vinegar, mustard, and the reserved leek cooking liquid until the mixture looks creamy. Drizzle it over the hot leeks and serve straightaway.

BUTTERY, NOT-QUITE-MUSHY BRUSSELS SPROUTS

Like most Brits, my fondness for sprouts goes way back. I like them every which way. When they're roasted and crispy. When they're cooked to a soft crunch in a pan with some fatty pork product. When they're boiled and lavishly buttered. When I was a girl, I even adored the sprouts a certain loving relative made in the pressure cooker, which turned gray and went so squishy that they collapsed in my mouth. I might not care to eat those today, but they certainly gave me an appreciation for sprouts cooked well past crunchy. Like these sprouts, which take a quick trip in boiling water before cooking slowly in quite a bit of butter. By the time they're done, they've absorbed that dairy flavor, the outer leaves have gone a little chewy and sticky, and the insides become soft—but not quite mushy.

Bring a medium pot of water to a boil and add enough kosher salt so it tastes a bit less salty than the sea. Add the sprouts and cook until they're still quite firm, but you can smoothly insert a knife into one while applying pressure, 6 to 7 minutes. Drain the sprouts well.

Melt the butter in a large skillet (wide enough for the Brussels sprouts to fit in a single layer) over medium-high heat, adjusting the heat so it bubbles away but doesn't brown. Add the sprouts to the butter, reduce the heat if necessary to cook at a rapid bubble, gently turning them over as they color, until they're very soft (but not mushy) and deep brown on the outsides, about 15 minutes—a bit more if you like them mushy.

Stir in the Maldon salt and use a slotted spoon to transfer the sprouts to a plate, leaving the remaining butter behind. Eat straightaway.

serves 4 to 6 as a side

Kosher salt

2 pounds large Brussels sprouts, bottoms trimmed and blemished outer leaves discarded

½ pound (2 sticks) unsalted butter, cut into a few pieces

1 teaspoon Maldon or another flaky sea salt

ROASTED CARROTS
WITH GARLIC CONFIT AND THYME

Just as a pork chop or veal breast might benefit from starting on the stovetop before being finished in the oven, so do carrots. Jumpstarting the browning on the stove helps bring out the carrots' sweetness. Then, once their flavor has concentrated in the oven and the carrots are fully and evenly tender—I'm not a fan of crunchy roasted carrots or those that are crispy outside and mushy inside—your job is done. The addition of butter, thyme, garlic, and just enough lemon to perk up the palate is just the whipped cream on the pudding. When the carrots no longer scald your fingers, you can eat them with your hands, occasionally nabbing a garlic clove and squeezing the skin so the soft, sweet flesh pops into your mouth.

Put the garlic cloves in a small pot and add just enough olive oil to completely cover them. Set the pot over medium heat and wait until you hear a quiet sizzle. Reduce the heat to low. Continue to cook the cloves until they are smooshably soft, 30 to 45 minutes. Remove the cloves and measure out 2 tablespoons of the oil (the rest of the slightly garlicky oil will keep in an airtight container in the fridge for up to 1 month).

Position a rack in the center of the oven and preheat to 500°F. Add the 2 tablespoons of garlic oil to an ovenproof skillet just big enough to hold the carrots in one layer and set the pan over high heat. When the oil smokes lightly, add the carrots, sprinkle on the salt, and use tongs to toss the carrots well. Cook, shaking and turning over the carrots occasionally, until they're browned in spots, 6 to 8 minutes.

Add the butter to the pan, let it melt, and toss the carrots well. Add the garlic cloves, skin and all, and pop the pan in the oven. After a few minutes, add the thyme to the pan. Toss, then continue to roast, tossing once more, until the carrots are evenly tender, 10 to 15 minutes, depending on the size of your carrots.

Gently squeeze on just enough lemon juice to add brightness, but not acidity. Let the carrots cool a bit and serve warm.

½ cup medium garlic cloves (about 16), unpeeled

About ⅔ cup extra-virgin olive oil

20 small carrots (the size of pointer fingers), scrubbed well but unpeeled and all but ½ inch of the tops removed

1 teaspoon Maldon or another flaky sea salt

1 tablespoon unsalted butter

4 thyme sprigs

½ lemon

SPICED CARROTS WITH YOGURT

They bring back memories, these carrots. I used to serve them at the first incarnation of the John Dory, which Ken Friedman and I opened in 2008 before closing, rethinking, and reopening in the Ace Hotel a couple years later. All is well now, but the closing was a sad time and one that's still hard for me to think about. Perhaps that's why I haven't served these carrots at any of my restaurants since, even though I love them so. The magic is in the way they're cut and cooked: slow cooking pieces with especially sharp edges means that not only do the carrots get good and sweet, but that those pointed edges get soft and fall off, mingling with the spices and yogurt to create a sort of coating for each carrot chunk. I add a spot of orange blossom water, which gives a whisper of flavor and aroma that you sense at the very beginning of each bite and again at the very end.

Combine the coriander and cumin seeds in a small pan, set the pan over medium-low heat, and cook, shaking and tossing frequently, until the spices are very fragrant and smoke lightly, about 5 minutes. Transfer them to a bowl or plate to cool slightly, then grind them to a coarse powder in a spice grinder or mortar. Add the cardamom seeds and grind or pound to a fine powder.

Starting at the tapered end of each carrot, cut a piece on the diagonal that's about 1 inch long, roll the carrot a quarter turn, cut another piece at the same angle, and so on. Heat 3 tablespoons of the oil in a medium pot (wide enough to hold the carrots snugly in more or less one layer) over high heat until it smokes lightly. Add the garlic and cook, stirring frequently, until it goes golden brown at the edges, about 1 minute.

Add the carrots, chile, ground spices, and salt to the pot and have a good old stir. Cover the pot, lower the heat to medium, and cook, stirring and later scraping the bottom occasionally, until the spices begin to stick to the pot, about 15 minutes. Add ¼ cup plus 2 tablespoons of water, stir, and cover the pot again.

serves 4 to 6 as a side

2 teaspoons coriander seeds

1 teaspoon cumin seeds

About 12 green cardamom pods, whacked with the flat of a chef's knife, pods discarded, seeds reserved (heaping ¼ teaspoon seeds)

2½ pounds medium carrots without greens (about 10), peeled, topped, and tailed

4 tablespoons extra-virgin olive oil, plus a drizzle for finishing

3 large garlic cloves, thinly sliced

1 red Thai or another small, very spicy fresh chile, thinly sliced (including seeds)

2 teaspoons Maldon or another flaky sea salt

3 tablespoons Greek yogurt

2 teaspoons orange blossom water (preferably Al Wadi brand)

A small handful of delicate cilantro sprigs, roughly chopped

A five-finger pinch of mint leaves (preferably black mint), roughly chopped at the last minute

Keep cooking, stirring occasionally, just until the carrots are fully tender but not mushy, about 25 minutes. After 10 minutes or so and occasionally thereafter, spend 30 seconds or so using a sturdy whisk or wooden spoon to very roughly stir and strike the carrots, not to smash the pieces but just to knock off some of the points that have gotten soft. If, along the way, the bits that end up stuck to the bottom of the pot turn dark brown, reduce the heat.

Take the pot off the heat and stir in the remaining 1 tablespoon of the oil, 1 tablespoon of the yogurt, the orange blossom water, and the herbs. Season to taste with salt. Transfer the carrots to a bowl. Add the remaining yogurt in little dollops on top along with another drizzle of olive oil.

VEGETABLE CRISPS WITH RED ZA'ATAR

At the end of a long winter, even my enthusiasm for root vegetables begins to flag a bit. And I'm an avowed root veg lover. That's when I turn to these colorful crisps, which make of the same old carrots and beets something special and fun. They're the most delicious things, these crisps. Every single one has its own character. Nibble a few at a time and you can still taste the earthy potato, the sweet beet. Not to mention they're very cute. Particularly the parsnips, which when sliced into rounds, fry up like little flowers.

While they're well worth the effort, crisps do require time and attention. Take care to slice the vegetables uniformly, applying even pressure as you work the mandoline. (In case you're afraid for your fingers, buy a few extra veg so you're not compelled to tempt fate.) The frying is quite simple, easier than many home cooks assume, though you'll want to make sure to tweak the heat if necessary and not overload the oil with veg, in order to maintain a consistent temperature. Once you master frying, you'll find yourself having a go with vegetables you didn't plan to fry. That's how I discovered fried beet leaves, which get a little lemony, almost like chard.

Using the mandoline, slice the parsnip, carrot, and beets into uniformly thin (you're shooting for about 1/16 inch) pieces. Cut the parsnip into round slices and the carrot and beets into lengthwise slices. You might want to halve the carrots and beets lengthwise before slicing to make it easier to slice evenly. Five minutes or so before you're ready to fry, slice the potatoes lengthwise, put them in a bowl of water, and gently toss with your hands to wash off some of the starch. Leave the potatoes in the bowl until you're ready to fry, but don't keep them in the water for more than 5 minutes or they will absorb too much water, making it difficult to fry them properly. Remove the thick center vein from the reserved beet leaves and tear the leaves into large pieces. Keep each type of vegetable separate.

serves 4 to 8
as a snack

SPECIAL EQUIPMENT

A mandoline; an electric deep-fryer or a large, heavy pot, a deep-fry thermometer, a splatter screen; and a spider

1 medium parsnip (about 1/4 pound), peeled, topped, and tailed

1 large carrot (about 1/2 pound), peeled, topped, tailed, and halved crosswise

3 golf-ball-size beets, unpeeled, trimmed of roots and all but 1 inch of stems, pert leaves reserved

9 fingerling potatoes, unpeeled (about 1/2 pound)

Peanut, sunflower, or vegetable oil for deep-frying

Kosher salt

About 5 tablespoons Red Za'atar Spice (page 239)

Add the oil (the amount depends on your fryer's capacity) to your electric deep-fryer and heat to 350°F. Alternatively, clip a deep-fry thermometer to a heavy pot and add at least 3 inches of oil. Heat the oil over high heat until it has reached 350°F. Line a large mixing bowl with paper towels for draining.

Drain the potatoes, pat them dry, and fry them in batches (a good handful at a time), using a long spoon to keep them moving in the oil so they fry evenly and tweaking the heat as necessary to maintain the temperature as best you can. Fry until they're light golden brown and crispy, about 5 minutes. As each batch is done, use the fryer basket or a spider to transfer it to the paper towel–lined bowl. Immediately give the vegetables a gentle toss to help drain the oil, season with kosher salt, and transfer to a serving bowl.

Lower the heat to bring the oil temperature to a steady 325°F. One type at a time, fry the rest of the vegetables in batches the same way you fried the potatoes, until they're crispy. Fry the beets last, because they'll stain the oil. The frying will take about 3 minutes for the parsnips, about 5 minutes for the carrots, 1 minute for the beet leaves, and about 4 minutes for the beets. You'll want to add the cover to the electric fryer or use a splatter screen when you're frying the leaves, because they splatter.

The crisps will stay crispy for up to 1 hour. When you're ready to eat, sprinkle on the za'atar and serve straightaway.

vegetables

and cream

{a love affair}

JANSSON'S TEMPTATION

No one can quite agree on who Jansson was. Yet I understand why he'd be tempted by this classic Swedish casserole of potatoes and cream. The traditional version includes pickled anchovy-like fish called sprats, but where I first encountered the dish—at Kensington Place—the chef, Rowley Leigh, used salted anchovies. I was smitten by the way they melded with the cream. I even like adding a few extra whole fillets to the baking dish right before popping it into the oven. As the whole thing bakes, the cream thickens, intensifying the umami quality of the anchovy. I add fennel to my version, which provides a meaty counterpoint to the velvety potatoes. The breadcrumbs on top add crunch and a sneaky pop of chile. The whole thing is so rich you only need a little, but so good that you want quite a lot.

Bring a medium pot of water to a boil over high heat and season it with kosher salt until it tastes a little less salty than the sea.

Cut the potatoes into approximately 3 x 1-inch wedges, then briefly rinse them under water and drain them. Add the potatoes to the boiling water, let the water return to a boil, and cook for about 4 minutes.

Meanwhile, halve the fennel bulbs lengthwise and cut each half through the root nub (so the wedges stay intact) into approximately 1-inch-thick wedges. Cut the onion through the root nub into approximately ½-inch-thick wedges.

When the 4 minutes have passed, add the fennel, let the water return to a boil, and cook just until both the potato and fennel are cooked through (you should be able to insert a sharp knife with only slight resistance), about 2 minutes or so. Transfer them to a colander and drain well.

Wipe the pot clean, add ¼ cup of the oil and the butter, and set the pot over medium-low heat. Once the butter melts, add the onion, halved garlic, anchovies, lemon zest, thyme, and ground fennel. Have a stir,

serves 8 to 10 as a side

Kosher salt

2 pounds large Yukon Gold potatoes (about 4), peeled

2 large fennel bulbs, stalks and outermost layer discarded, tender fronds reserved, root end trimmed of brown bits

1 large Spanish onion (about 1 pound), peeled, root end trimmed but left intact, halved through the root nub

¼ cup plus 2 tablespoons extra-virgin olive oil

2 tablespoons unsalted butter

13 medium garlic cloves, 12 halved lengthwise, 1 finely grated on a rasp-style grater

7 salt-packed whole anchovies, soaked and filleted (see page 13)

4 strips (about 4 x ½ inch) lemon zest

4 thyme sprigs

1 teaspoon fennel seeds, ground or pounded to a powder

4 cups heavy cream

cover the pot, and cook, stirring now and again, until the onions are very soft but not colored, about 20 minutes.

Position a rack in the center of the oven and preheat to 450°F.

Add the cream and 1 tablespoon of the Maldon salt to the pot and raise the heat to medium-high. Bring the cream to a boil, scraping off any anchovy stuck to the sides of the pot. Lower the heat and simmer for 5 minutes. Add the potatoes and fennel and raise the heat to medium-high again. Bring the cream to a boil, then turn off the heat. Discard the lemon peel and thyme stems.

Use a slotted spoon to transfer the potato, fennel, and onion to a large, heavy enameled baking dish so they're evenly distributed and in more or less one layer. Pour the cream mixture over the vegetables and give the dish a gentle shake to distribute it evenly. Bake, uncovered, until the cream has thickened slightly and browned in spots, about 25 minutes.

Meanwhile, roughly chop some of the reserved fennel fronds. Working in batches so as not to overload your food processor, add the bread and a five-finger pinch of the fennel fronds (saving the remaining fronds for garnish), then pulse until you have very coarse breadcrumbs (a mixture of pebbly bits and chunks, ½ inch at the largest). Transfer the crumbs to a mixing bowl, add the remaining 2 tablespoons of oil, the grated garlic, a pinch of salt, the Parmesan, and the chiles, then give it a good old mix with your hands.

Remove the dish from the oven and sprinkle the breadcrumbs evenly over the top. Turn on the broiler and return the dish to the oven or broiler drawer. Broil, rotating the pan occasionally, until the breadcrumbs go golden brown and crispy, 5 to 10 minutes.

Let the casserole cool for a few minutes, then grab another five-finger pinch of the fronds and sprinkle it over the top. Have at it.

1 tablespoon plus a pinch of Maldon or another flaky sea salt

½ pound slightly stale rustic bread, such as filone, crust discarded, pulled into about 1-inch pieces (about 2½ cups)

1 ounce Parmesan cheese, finely grated

10 dried pequín chiles, crumbled, or pinches of red pepper flakes

MORELS WITH MADEIRA CREAM ON TOAST

I wouldn't be much of an Englishwoman if I didn't fancy mushrooms on toast. This is a luxurious version, made with meaty, woodsy morels lavished with cream. Madeira lends its nutty complexity to the dish and cuts the richness with its acidity.

Morels can be spendy, so feel free to bulk up ¼ pound with cremini or oyster mushrooms. If you're itching for morels but it's not quite spring, you can get away with using the high-quality dried version. To get the right amount for this recipe, soak 2 ounces of dried morels in 2 cups of warm water for half an hour, then squeeze them gently to rid them of excess water.

Melt the butter in a medium pot over high heat until it froths. Add the shallots and salt, stir, and reduce the heat to medium-low. Cook, stirring, just until the shallots have a kiss of brown, about 3 minutes. Stir in the morels and cook, stirring now and then, until the mushrooms are just cooked through, about 5 minutes.

Add the stock, cream, ⅓ cup of the Madeira, and the tarragon. Raise the heat to high, bring to a boil, and cook, stirring occasionally, just until the liquid has thickened slightly, about 3 minutes. Pour in the remaining ⅓ cup of the Madeira and continue to boil until the liquid thickens just enough to coat the back of a spoon, about 2 minutes. Stir in the crème fraîche and take the pot off the heat.

Toast the bread just until the surface is crispy, then rub the cut sides of the garlic on the surface of each slice. Divide the toast among 4 plates, spoon on the mushrooms, and sprinkle on the remaining tarragon.

serves 4 as a side

3 tablespoons unsalted butter

1 large shallot, finely chopped (about ¼ cup)

1 teaspoon Maldon or another flaky sea salt

Scant ½ pound fresh morel mushrooms, halved lengthwise if large and cleaned (see "Cleaning Wild Mushrooms," page 135)

⅔ cup Simple Chicken Stock (page 245)

⅔ cup heavy cream

⅔ cup dry Madeira (preferably special reserve)

A five-finger pinch of tarragon leaves, roughly chopped, plus more for finishing

1 tablespoon crème fraîche

4 thick slices crusty country bread

1 medium garlic clove, halved

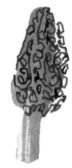

CREAMED SPINACH

If you've made it this far in the book, you can probably tell I'm partial to a bit of cream. But my version of creamed spinach is—surprisingly, perhaps—more about highlighting the earthy, lemony flavor and slightly meaty texture of this underappreciated green. White wine and lemon zest keep the dish's richness from becoming heavy. And the anchovies provide sneaky complexity: no one will know they're there unless you tell.

In a large, wide pot, bring ½ cup of water to a boil over high heat. Add the spinach (in batches if necessary) and pop on a lid. Cook until the spinach at the bottom wilts, about 2 minutes. Stir well and keep cooking with the lid on until all the spinach is fully wilted but not cooked to buggery, about 2 minutes more. Drain the spinach in a colander, pressing the spinach with a wooden spoon to squeeze out some of the water. Spread the spinach on a large plate so it doesn't carry on cooking and let it cool to the touch, then squeeze the spinach to remove as much water as you can.

Wipe out the pot. Pour in 3 tablespoons of the oil and heat it over medium heat until it shimmers. Add the shallots and ½ teaspoon of the salt and cook, stirring occasionally, until translucent, about 3 minutes. Stir in the garlic and cook until it's lightly golden at the edges, about 2 minutes. Stir in the thyme and cook until the shallots are soft and shrink a bit, about 3 minutes more. Push the shallot-garlic mixture to the side, add the anchovies to the oil on the empty side, and cook without stirring until they're lightly browned, about 2 minutes. Stir the anchovies and vegetables together.

Pour in the white wine, increase the heat to high, and bring it to a boil. Boil until the wine has reduced so that it just barely covers the bottom of the pan, 3 to 5 minutes. Pour in the cream, let it come to a boil, and cook, stirring occasionally, until the mixture thickens enough to coat the back of a metal spoon, 5 to 7 minutes. Sprinkle

serves 4 to 6 as a side

2¼ pounds hearty spinach (not baby), all but 1 inch of stems trimmed

4 tablespoons extra-virgin olive oil

2 large shallots (a generous ¼ pound), cut into thin rings

1½ teaspoons Maldon or another flaky sea salt

2 medium garlic cloves, thinly sliced

1 tablespoon thyme leaves, finely chopped

3 salt-packed whole anchovies, soaked and filleted (see page 13)

1 cup white wine

1½ cups heavy cream

¼ teaspoon finely grated lemon zest

Several gratings of nutmeg

Several turns of freshly ground black pepper

in the spinach, unfurling the clumps as you add it to the pot, and cook, stirring often, until it's hot through, about 3 minutes.

Stir in the lemon zest, nutmeg, and pepper along with the remaining 1 tablespoon of oil and 1 teaspoon of salt. Cook, stirring, just until the spinach is fully tender but retains its integrity and the flavors come together, about 3 minutes. Eat straightaway.

SWEET CORN ICE CREAM WITH BUTTERSCOTCH

When I was first served corn ice cream, I thought the guy who made it was having a laugh. To me, corn meant succotash, soup, and steamy ears buttered and sprinkled with crunchy sea salt. It did not mean dessert. Yet while it took me a good minute to get my head around the idea, it took me only about five seconds to eat every last bit. Of course, corn ice cream makes perfect sense—corn is good mates with dairy and during summer, the veg is sweeter than strawberries, peaches, and other fruits commonly spotted in ice cream. A healthy drizzle of butterscotch and a scattering of caramel popcorn add sweet-salty complexity and crunch.

make the butterscotch

Combine the cream, Scotch, and salt in a measuring cup with a spout. Use a knife to scrape the seeds of the vanilla bean into the cup and stir well.

Combine the granulated sugar, butter, brown sugar, corn syrup, and ¼ cup of water in a medium saucepan with high sides. Set it over high heat and bring to a boil. Attach a candy thermometer to the pan and boil until the mixture reaches 245°F. Remove the pan from the heat and gradually whisk in the cream mixture. Let the mixture cool to room temperature. You'll have about 1 cup of butterscotch.

Use straightaway or stir once more and keep in an airtight container in the fridge for up to 2 weeks. Gently reheat until warm before using.

make the ice cream

Cut the corn kernels from the cobs, reserving the cobs. Cut the cobs crosswise into a few pieces. Combine the kernels and cobs in a medium pot along with the cream, milk, salt, and ¼ cup of the sugar. Bring the liquid to a simmer, stirring occasionally, over medium-high heat, then turn off the heat, cover the pot, and let the mixture steep at room temperature for at least 2 hours or in the fridge for as long as 12 hours. Remove the cobs, gently scraping them with a spoon to get

makes about 1½ pints plus ¾ cup of butterscotch

SPECIAL EQUIPMENT

A 1½-quart-capacity ice cream maker and a candy thermometer

FOR THE BUTTERSCOTCH

3 tablespoons heavy cream

1 tablespoon Scotch

1 teaspoon Maldon or another flaky sea salt

¼ vanilla bean, split lengthwise

¼ cup plus 1½ tablespoons granulated sugar

4 tablespoons (½ stick) unsalted butter

2 tablespoons packed light brown sugar

1½ teaspoons light corn syrup

FOR THE ICE CREAM

3 medium ears corn, shucked

2 cups heavy cream

1 cup whole milk

(continued on next page)

at any liquid that may be hiding in them, and discard the cobs. Strain the remaining mixture through a sieve into a clean medium pot, stirring and pressing on the kernels to release as much corn flavor as possible. Discard the kernels.

Bring the milk mixture to a simmer over medium heat and turn off the heat. Combine the egg yolks and the remaining ½ cup of sugar in a medium mixing bowl and whisk until smooth. Slowly but steadily add about ¾ cup of the milk mixture to the yolk mixture, whisking constantly. Then slowly but steadily add the yolk mixture to the pot, again whisking constantly. Cook over medium-low heat, whisking constantly and adjusting the heat if necessary to maintain a simmer, until the mixture thickens enough to coat the back of a spoon, about 10 minutes.

Strain the mixture again through a sieve into a medium mixing bowl, pressing and then discarding the solids. Fill a larger bowl halfway with very icy water and nestle the medium bowl inside. Stir frequently until the mixture is cold. Cover the medium bowl and chill in the fridge for at least 4 hours or overnight.

Pour the mixture into an ice cream maker and process according to the manufacturer's instructions. Transfer the ice cream to an airtight container and freeze until firm. Serve straightaway or keep the ice cream in the freezer for up to 3 days.

When you're ready to eat, scoop the ice cream into bowls, drizzle on some butterscotch, and top with some of the caramel popcorn.

¼ teaspoon kosher salt

¾ cup granulated sugar

6 large egg yolks

FOR SERVING
Caramel Popcorn with Nuts (page 246), optional

American corn, whether it's white, yellow, or bicolored, is some of the best you can eat: not just candy sweet but full of flavor. Truly lovely corn is one of the pleasures I hadn't experienced until I came to the States.

Selecting corn can be a bit difficult: pesky husks hide the rows of kernels underneath, so how are you to tell if you've got a good ear? I get a bit grumpy when I see people at the market tearing husks off corn like they own the ears. That's a bit bold, isn't it? The better way is to look for ears whose husks hug the kernels tight. I don't mind if there's a little brown on the silk peeking out at the tip. Run your hands along the husk, feeling the kernels underneath. Not only should the kernels feel nice and firm, none of them dented or missing, but they should also run all the way to the top of the cob. Once you buy your corn, cook it straightaway. Like peas, corn gets starchier and starchier and less and less sweet once picked.

Corn shows up in soup and pudding and pasta in this book. Yet when I have an armful of ears from the market, I'll often go an even simpler route. I'll leave the husks on and soak the corn in a bucket of water for about 15 minutes. I'll get some coals glowing hot and lay the ears directly on the grill grates, husk and all, so the kernels steam. When the husks begin to burn away, the fire licks the kernels and adds a kiss of smokiness. This usually takes 10 to 15 minutes. (If the kernels shrivel up at all, though, it's been too long.) Next, I strip off the husks, rub the corn with butter, and sprinkle on salt and perhaps a little lemon juice. Oh—and I always make sure that butter is soft. The softer it is, the faster I get to eat the corn.

Three vegetable juices

When I crave vegetables as a snack rather than as part of a meal, I either gnaw on a carrot or break out my juicer. Vegetable juices are healthy, sure, but I love them for the same reason I do butter and cream, kidneys and marrow: because they taste great. Invest in a high-quality juicer, like a Breville (and the masticating kind if you like green juice), and use these three recipes as jumping-off points. You might want to add a sneaky bit of jalapeño or garlic, or mess around with the proportions to suit your tastes. Tweak them all you want, just promise you'll drink them cold, cold, cold. They're so refreshing that way.

MY FAVORITE GREEN JUICE

serves 2

Generous ¼ pound Tuscan kale (about 6 large leaves), very bottoms of stems trimmed, roughly chopped

¼ pound Swiss chard (about 6 large leaves with stems), very bottoms of stems trimmed, roughly chopped

1 green apple (about ½ pound), washed well, unpeeled, cored, and cut into pieces to fit in your juicer

2 large celery stalks, very bottoms trimmed, roughly chopped

A five-finger pinch of basil leaves

A five-finger pinch of mint leaves

A five-finger pinch of delicate flat-leaf parsley sprigs

2 teaspoons lemon juice

Pinch of Maldon or another flaky sea salt

Juice all the ingredients, except the lemon and salt, according to the manufacturer's instructions. To get the maximum amount of juice, you might want to alternate feeding greens and apple through the juicer. Skim off most of the foam. Stir in the lemon juice and salt until the salt dissolves. Pour the juice into two ice-filled glasses and drink straightaway.

CARROT-ORANGE JUICE WITH GINGER AND CILANTRO

serves 2

Scant 1 pound carrots (about 2 large), well scrubbed, unpeeled

½ ounce ginger (a 1 x 1-inch knob), washed well, unpeeled

A five-finger pinch of delicate cilantro sprigs

3 tennis-ball-size oranges, halved and squeezed through a strainer into a bowl

One ingredient by one, feed the carrots, ginger, and cilantro through the juicer. Combine the carrot juice mixture with the orange juice and stir well. Pour into two ice-filled glasses and drink straightaway.

BEET-APPLE JUICE

serves 2

Scant 1 pound beets (about 4 medium), washed well, unpeeled, and cut into pieces to fit in your juicer

1 green apple (about ½ pound), washed well, unpeeled, cored, and cut into pieces to fit in your juicer

Feed the beets through the juicer, then the apple. Pour the juice into two ice-filled glasses and drink straightaway.

Sauces, dressings,
     pickles, and friends

✵ Kimchi ✵

ferment in the fridge
for 2-4 weeks

CABBAGE KIMCHI

Vicky Oh used to be a kitchen assistant at Salvation Taco. Her family runs its own kimchi company, Arirang, which makes a very tasty version of the pickled vegetable that is Korea's national dish. For my Steamed and Raw Radish Salad with Kimchi and Sesame (page 87), I'll often use a jar of Arirang kimchi. But I got curious about the process of making it myself and just had to have a go at it. I based this recipe on one Vicky shared with me. Turns out it's good fun, slathering a paste of sticky-rice flour, salted shrimp, and ground Korean chile on cabbage leaves and scrunching the heads—particularly when you enlist some friends to help. My theory on kimchi is that if you go through the task of making it, you might as well end up with a lot. Once it's ready, you can give those friends a jar for their efforts.

I like tasting the kimchi at different stages, from the time it's fresh and crunchy all the way until it gets funky and even a bit fizzy. I also like including other farmers' market finds, from all types of radishes to cucumbers to garlic scapes.

Put the cabbage in a big bowl and sprinkle the salt in between the cabbage leaves. Cover and keep in the fridge overnight.

The next day, remove the cabbage from the fridge and drain it well.

Combine the rice flour and 1½ cups of water in a small pot, whisk until smooth, then set the pot over medium-low heat. Cook, whisking constantly, until the mixture thickens to a loose sludge, 1 to 2 minutes. Take the pot off the heat and let the mixture cool to room temperature.

Combine the gochugaru, garlic, ginger, salted shrimp, sugar, and rice flour mixture in a food processor and process until the mixture is smooth. Put the chile paste in a very large mixing bowl along with the daikon and scallions. Use gloved hands to mix all three together very well.

Take one of the cabbage quarters and add it to the bowl. Using gloved hands again, slather the vegetable-chile mixture all over the cab-

makes about 5 quarts

SPECIAL EQUIPMENT

A pair of disposable food prep gloves and 3 wide-mouth 2-quart glass or plastic containers with airtight lids, cleaned well

2 large heads napa cabbage, bottoms trimmed but kept intact, outermost leaves discarded, and quartered lengthwise

About 2 tablespoons Maldon or another flaky sea salt

¼ cup sweet rice flour (also called sticky rice or glutinous rice flour)

1½ to 2 cups gochugaru (Korean chile flakes)

¾ cup peeled garlic cloves (about 20)

2 ounces fresh ginger (a 3 x 1½-inch knob), peeled and very roughly sliced

½ cup jarred Korean salted shrimp (from the refrigerated section of Korean markets)

¼ cup granulated sugar

(continued on next page)

bage, spreading it on and between the leaves. Tuck an especially healthy amount into the spaces between the leaves near the bottom of the cabbage. Once the entire cabbage quarter has a red tint, move on to the next one.

Fold the cabbage quarters onto themselves to create tight bundles and divide them among the containers, firmly pressing so they sit tight and leaving at least 1 inch of space between the cabbage and the jars' openings. Divide any remaining chile-vegetable mixture among the jars. Press down firmly on the cabbage again to minimize air pockets that might be hiding out.

Seal the jars tightly with the lids and leave them at room temperature overnight. You might want to set them on plates to catch any liquid that sneaks out of the lids as the kimchi ferments. You can nibble on the kimchi at this point, when it's fresh, or keep it in the fridge and eat it after 2 to 4 weeks when it's good and funky. If necessary, occasionally press down on the cabbage with a clean spoon to make sure it's covered by liquid. It'll keep for up to several months.

2 pounds daikon radish, peeled, topped, tailed, and cut into 3 x ⅛-inch matchsticks

1 pound scallions (about 5 bunches), roots trimmed, whites and greens trimmed of ugly bits, cut into 1-inch lengths

{ the kimchi squat }

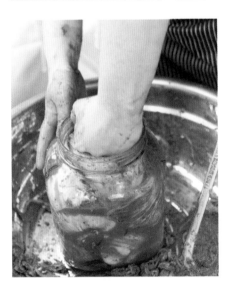

GIARDINIERA

From the Italian word for gardener, *giardiniera* refers to this pickle, a garden's worth of vegetables in a simple brine. The different textures and flavors they provide make for an exciting pickle. The particular vegetables and proportions are ultimately up to you, but I do urge you to seek out Castelvetrano olives, which are fleshy and not too salty. They keep the giardiniera nice and fresh. Serve it for nibbling with drinks or as part of an antipasti plate. Or finely chop the vegetables, mix in a little dill, and spoon it onto hot dogs or sausages, along with a little mustard. The giardiniera keeps in the fridge for a few weeks, but if you like pickles, they won't last that long before they disappear.

Combine the kosher salt and 8 cups of cold water in a large container and stir to dissolve the salt. Add 1 cup of ice cubes, then the bell peppers, celery, carrot, onion, cauliflower, radishes, garlic, and chiles. Cover and store in the fridge overnight or up to 24 hours.

Drain the vegetables, discarding the water, and rinse them briefly under running water. Drain them very well and pat them dry.

Meanwhile, combine the sugar and 1¾ cups of water in a small pot and set it over medium heat. Cook, stirring frequently, just until the sugar dissolves. Transfer the mixture to a large bowl and add the vinegar, olives, olive brine, oil, oregano, and red pepper flakes.

If you have a jar large enough to hold the liquid and vegetables as well as space for the jar in your fridge, go ahead and combine everything in the jar. If not, divide the liquid and vegetables between several tall containers with tight-fitting lids, making sure the liquid covers the veg.

Let it pickle in the fridge for at least 1 week or up to 3 weeks before you eat it. I like it cold or at room temperature. Stir well before you eat.

makes about 2 quarts

1 cup kosher salt

2 medium red bell peppers, seeded and deribbed, cut into 1-inch pieces

2 medium celery stalks, topped, tailed, and cut on the diagonal into ¼-inch-thick slices

1 medium carrot, cut into irregular 1-inch pieces

1 medium red onion (about ½ pound), root trimmed but left intact, peeled, and cut into 8 wedges through the root nub

1 cup small (about 1 inch) cauliflower florets

1 cup trimmed medium red radishes, halved lengthwise

1 large head garlic, unpeeled and halved crosswise

2 medium jalapeño chiles, sliced into ¼-inch-thick rings (including seeds)

2 tablespoons granulated sugar

4¾ cups champagne vinegar or white wine vinegar

1 cup roughly chopped pitted Castelvetrano olives, plus ½ cup of their brine

½ cup extra-virgin olive oil

1 tablespoon dried oregano

2 teaspoons red pepper flakes

SPICY DILL PICKLES

At home—unlike in restaurants or on farms—you don't often find your-self flush with barrels of cucumbers that need to be preserved in the cupboard for months and months. So these pickles don't require can-ning jars or sterilizing, because they're meant to last just a few weeks in the refrigerator. This means they're a bit simpler to make. They provide everything you want in a pickle: they're assertively salty and sour, with just a spot of sugar (but not sweetness) for balance. They're plenty crunchy, too—what a shame it would be to lose the texture that makes Kirby cucumbers so good. To that end, always start with cucum-bers that are no less than perfect, firm and unblemished. The pickle jar isn't meant to hide rubbish vegetables but rather to preserve nice ones. And don't toss the brine once you've eaten all the pickles. While the pickles are the main event, the flavorful brine makes a fine chaser for a shot of whiskey.

Combine the vinegar, salt, sugar, coriander seeds, fennel seeds, mus-tard seeds, and 2 cups of water in a medium pot. Set the pot over high heat and bring to a boil, stirring occasionally, until the salt and sugar have dissolved. Remove the mixture from the heat and let it fully cool.

Put the cucumbers, onion, garlic, chiles, dill, thyme and bay leaves in a 2-quart jar or divide them among two tall 1-quart jars. Pour in just enough of the vinegar mixture to cover the cucumbers (you might have a little liquid left over), doing your best to distribute the corian-der, fennel, and mustard seeds evenly if you're using more than one container.

Cover with an airtight lid and let the cucumbers pickle in the fridge for at least 1 week, or even better 2 weeks, before you eat them. They'll keep for another 2 weeks in the fridge. I like to eat them cold or at room temperature.

makes about 2 quarts

3 cups distilled white vinegar

½ cup kosher salt

3 tablespoons granulated sugar

1 tablespoon coriander seeds

1 tablespoon fennel seeds

1 tablespoon yellow mustard seeds

10 small Kirby cucumbers (about 5 x 1½ inches), halved lengthwise

½ medium Spanish onion, cut into ¼-inch-thick slices

4 medium garlic cloves, peeled

9 dried red Thai chiles, or arbol chiles

3 large dill sprigs

1 large thyme sprig

3 fresh bay leaves

PICCALILLI

Food lore has it that piccalilli started as Brits having a go at making achar, Indian-style pickles. I suppose that accounts for the turmeric and ginger. Otherwise, I think we might've missed the target. Personally, I like to think of piccalilli as England's answer to bread and butter pickles. Piccalilli has a similar sweet and sour quality, which I just love. As a kid, I'd dump it on my butter-slathered cheese sandwiches, eat it with sausage rolls or a ploughman's, and wolf it straight from the jar with yellow-stained fingers. My favorite bit was crunching on the pearl onions, so tiny and perfect. Today I'll still have it on cheese sandwiches made with sharp, funky cheddar, or alongside pâté or boiled ham.

Combine the salt and 8 cups of water in a large container and stir to dissolve the salt. Add the cauliflower, cucumbers, and onions. Cover and store in the fridge overnight or up to 24 hours.

Drain the vegetables, discarding the water, and rinse them briefly under running water. Let the vegetables sit in the colander for 10 minutes or so, so they drain really well.

Meanwhile, combine the vinegar, sugar, mustard powder, and ground ginger in a medium pot. Bring the mixture to a boil over high heat, stirring to dissolve the sugar and spices, then add the vegetables, let the liquid come to a simmer, and lower the heat to maintain a gentle simmer. Cook just until the onions turn bubblegum pink and they give slightly when you squeeze them, about 4 minutes. Drain the vegetables in a sieve set over a large bowl, reserving the liquid, and return the liquid to the pot.

Bring the liquid to a boil once more, whisk in the flour and turmeric, and whisk for a minute or so. Working in batches, blend the mixture (be careful when blending hot liquids) until smooth.

makes 2 generous quarts

1 cup kosher salt

1 small head cauliflower, cut into 1½-inch florets (about 3 cups)

5 medium Kirby cucumbers or other small crunchy cucumbers without big seeds, peeled and cut into irregularly shaped 1½-inch pieces (about 4 cups)

2 cups red pearl onions (about 10 ounces), soaked in warm water, peeled, and trimmed of any tough bits

6 cups distilled white vinegar

½ cup granulated sugar

1 tablespoon mustard powder (preferably Colman's)

1 teaspoon ground ginger

½ cup all-purpose flour

3½ tablespoons ground turmeric

If you have a jar large enough to hold the liquid and vegetables as well as space for the jar in your fridge, go ahead and combine everything in the jar. If not, divide the liquid and vegetables among several tall containers with tight-fitting lids, making sure the liquid covers the veg. Let everything cool fully, then cover with the lids and refrigerate.

Let the piccalilli pickle in the fridge for at least 2 days before you eat it. It keeps in the fridge for up to 3 weeks more. I like to eat it cold or at room temperature.

CARROT TOP PESTO

If you've never nibbled a carrot top, you have a happy surprise waiting for you. The greens are delicious: a little less carroty than the roots, and almost briny, like heartier borage. Arriving home from the market with not only a collection of sweet, colorful roots but also a big old tuft of bushy tops is like ordering pork shoulder and finding out that the kind butcher has snuck a couple of trotters into your bag.

I treat the tops as I would a tender herb, adding little sprigs to salads as I might parsley or dill. And because each bunch of carrots can bring twice the volume in tops, I make pesto. As much as I like the particular flavor of the tops themselves, I also like how they carry the flavor of basil, which comes through quite a bit considering how few leaves you use.

Combine the carrot tops and basil in a small food processor, pulse several times, then add the walnuts, Parmesan, garlic, and salt. Pulse several more times, add the oil, then process full-on, stopping and scraping down the sides of the processor or stirring gently if need be, until the mixture is well combined but still a bit chunky. Taste and season with more salt, if you fancy.

makes about 1 cup

4 cups lightly packed delicate carrot tops (stems discarded), roughly chopped

A small handful of basil leaves

½ cup walnut halves

1 ounce Parmesan cheese, finely grated

1 medium garlic clove, halved lengthwise

1 teaspoon Maldon or another flaky sea salt

½ cup extra-virgin olive oil

KALE PUREE

If it weren't for Kale Puree, I wouldn't be where I am today. I was still a young cook in England wondering what I'd do next when I saw Rose Gray and Ruth Rogers, chefs at London's River Café, on the telly. At the time, food TV wasn't all clever editing and pretty colors. Their show on the BBC just showed them, cooking. I watched them make this four-ingredient puree and toss it in a pan with some penne. They were accomplished chefs, but the food they were making wasn't complicated at all. I wanted to cook like that. So I called up River Café and talked my way into a try-out. I went on to work there, and Rose and Ruth became my mentors and friends. I'm grateful that they never tried my first go at the puree, which I made immediately after I switched off the telly. I used crap olive oil and it wasn't very good. Please don't make the mistake I did.

Put 4 of the garlic cloves in a medium pot, fill it with water, cover, and bring the water to a boil over high heat. Add enough kosher salt so that the water tastes slightly salty and add the kale, prodding to submerge it. Cook uncovered until the kale is tender and tears easily, 2 to 3 minutes.

Fish out the boiled garlic cloves from the pot and reserve them. Drain the kale in a colander and when it's cool enough to handle, squeeze out as much water as you can. Roughly chop the kale, the boiled garlic, and the raw garlic.

Combine the kale, garlic, and Maldon salt in a food processor. Process, stopping occasionally to prod and stir, for about 45 seconds, then add the oil and process, stirring once or twice, to a fairly smooth puree. Whenever I make this at one of my restaurants, I use a Vita-Prep to make the puree silky smooth, but I like a slightly coarse puree too.

The puree keeps in an airtight container in the fridge for up to 5 days.

makes 1 generous cup

5 medium garlic cloves, peeled

1 pound Tuscan kale, thick stems removed (about ½ pound after trimming)

Kosher salt

1 teaspoon Maldon or another flaky sea salt

½ cup extra-virgin olive oil

A NEAT TRICK FOR REMOVING KALE STEMS

Before I use kale or other leafy greens with woody stems, I often remove the thick stems. I've seen home cooks do this with a knife, which you can do if you fancy. I have a quicker way. Working one leaf at a time, firmly grab the end of the stem with one hand. With the other, use your thumb and index finger to firmly pinch together the bottom of the leaf on either side of the stem and pull away from the stem end, stripping off the leaves in one go.

GRILLED-VEGETABLE VINAIGRETTE

I like salads that keep you occupied, that give you something to search for and get excited about. This chunky dressing brings that pleasure to even the simplest salad. Thanks to the dressing, each bite of the salad is different. You might come across a sweet bit of fennel or onion in one bite, and a slightly bitter bit of Treviso in another. Bright with vinegar and herbs, the dressing also goes well spooned over a steak along with crumbled blue cheese or dolloped on a lamb chop with some feta.

Halve the fennel bulb lengthwise and cut each half through the root nub (so the wedges stay intact) into approximately 1-inch-thick wedges.

Heat a grill or heavy grill pan over high heat until it's good and hot, about 5 minutes. Reduce the heat to medium and add the fennel, onion, and Treviso. Cook, turning the vegetables over occasionally, until the fennel and onion are lightly charred in spots and cooked through, but still have a little bite, about 20 minutes. The Treviso is done when the stems are tender but still have a little bite, the leaves are wilty, the tips crackly, and the color has changed from magenta to sienna with dark brown edges, 15 to 20 minutes.

As they finish, pop the grilled vegetables into a bowl and cover with plastic wrap until they've cooled fully. They'll steam a bit and cook some more as they cool. Once they've all cooled, chop the vegetables into a mix of about ½-inch pieces, some smaller and some larger.

Pop the vegetables back into the bowl, add the oil, vinegar, salt, and garlic and stir really well. Toss the mint and marjoram together on a cutting board, give them a rough chop, and stir them into the dressing.

makes a scant 2 cups

1 medium fennel bulb, outer layer, stalks, and fronds removed, root end trimmed of brown bits

1 small red onion (about ¼ pound), cut into ½-inch-thick rounds

1 small head Treviso (a generous ¼ pound), outermost leaves removed, bottom trimmed of brown bits, quartered lengthwise, or a small head radicchio, prepped like the Treviso and cut into ½-inch-thick wedges

½ cup extra-virgin olive oil

3 tablespoons sherry vinegar

1 teaspoon Maldon or another flaky sea salt

1 small garlic clove, very finely chopped

A five-finger pinch of mint leaves (preferably black mint)

A five-finger pinch of marjoram leaves

SALAD CREAM

This creamy, tangy dressing is meant to mimic the jarred salad cream I grew up with in England, which I poured all over raw vegetables. I realize now that it's a lot like a really liquidy version of the deviled egg filling I make at The Spotted Pig, with a little tarragon thrown in. If you're making this for Salad Sandwiches (page 84), you might want to give some of the boiled egg whites a good old chop and pile them on the bread along with the soft-boiled eggs. No point in wasting.

Fill a medium pot at least halfway with water and bring it to a boil over high heat. Use a slotted spoon to gently add the eggs to the water, cook them for 10 minutes (set a timer), then run them under cold water until they're fully cool. Lightly tap each egg against the counter to crack the shell all over, then peel them, halve them lengthwise, and pop out the yolks. (Reserve the whites for another purpose, like Salad Sandwiches, or for nibbling.)

Use the back of a spoon to force the yolks through a mesh sieve into a food processor. Add the oil, cream, vinegar, mustard, garlic, salt, and 2 teaspoons of water and process until very smooth and creamy. Add the tarragon and process briefly. It keeps in an airtight container in the refrigerator for up to 2 days.

makes 1 generous cup

6 large eggs

¼ cup extra-virgin olive oil

¼ cup heavy cream

2 tablespoons red wine vinegar

1 tablespoon plus 1 teaspoon Dijon mustard

1 very small garlic clove, roughly chopped

1 teaspoon Maldon or another flaky sea salt

A small handful of tarragon leaves, roughly chopped

SIMPLE LEMON DRESSING

This all-purpose dressing brightens whatever it touches, like Snap Pea Salad (page 23) or Greek Salad (page 81). It proves that three modest ingredients can become something extra-special when they're combined in just the right proportions.

Combine the ingredients in a container with a tight-fitting lid and shake well until the mixture looks creamy. Taste and add a little more oil, lemon, or salt, if you'd like. Set it aside until you're ready to use it and shake again just before you do.

makes about ¾ cup

½ cup extra-virgin olive oil

¼ cup lemon juice

¾ teaspoon Maldon or another flaky sea salt

RED ZA'ATAR SPICE

Many Middle Eastern cooks have their own family recipe for this classic spice blend. This is my version. While some cooks use dried herbs and only a little sumac, I like to use fresh herbs, like thyme and marjoram, and lots of sumac, which gives the za'atar a pretty purplish red color and a refreshing lemony quality. The mixture is meant to season Vegetable Crisps (page 200), but it's also a fine thing to sprinkle on thick yogurt or douse with olive oil to make a dip for bread.

Toast the sesame seeds in a small dry skillet over medium-low heat, stirring and tossing almost constantly, just until they've turned a light golden color, 1 to 2 minutes. Transfer them to a bowl to cool.

Combine the sumac and herbs in a small food processor (or small spice grinder) and process to a fairly fine, slightly moist powder. Put the mixture in the bowl with the sesame seeds, add the salt, and stir well.

The za'atar keeps in an airtight container in the fridge for up to 5 days.

makes a generous ½ cup

1 tablespoon sesame seeds

¼ cup sumac

2 tablespoons very coarsely chopped marjoram leaves

2 tablespoons very coarsely chopped oregano leaves

2 tablespoons very coarsely chopped thyme leaves

½ teaspoon Maldon or another flaky sea salt

MY GARAM MASALA

Any Indian grocer and many supermarkets nowadays stock this spice mixture, which is a staple in Indian cooking. But premade versions aren't quite as nice as those you make yourself. When you toast and grind whole spices, the resulting mixture is especially lively and aromatic. While a spice grinder is much easier on your arm, I prefer using a mortar to make the coarse powder, because the smell of toasty pulverized spices is so invigorating. In fact, if you do, you might want to whack the cardamom pods with the flat of a chef's knife, discard the fibrous pods, and use just the seeds.

Combine the coriander, cumin, cardamom, cinnamon, chiles, mace, and cloves in a medium skillet. Set the pan over medium-low heat and cook, shaking and tossing frequently, until the spices are toasty and very fragrant, about 5 minutes. Transfer them to a bowl or plate to cool slightly, then grind them to a coarse powder in a spice grinder or pound them in a large mortar. Add the nutmeg, ground ginger, and bay leaves and grind or pound until you have a fairly fine powder. It's OK if the bay leaves are still in small pieces and not completely broken down.

Store the garam masala in an airtight container in a cool, dry place for up to 1 month.

makes a generous ½ cup

3 tablespoons coriander seeds

3 tablespoons cumin seeds

1 tablespoon green cardamom pods

2 small cinnamon sticks (about 3 inches each), roughly crumbled

10 dried pequín chiles, crumbled, or pinches of red pepper flakes

½ whole mace blade or 1 teaspoon pieces

2 teaspoons whole cloves

1½ tablespoons finely grated nutmeg (from about 2 small nutmegs)

2 teaspoons ground ginger

2 large fresh bay leaves, stems removed and leaves torn into small pieces

SIMPLE TOMATO SAUCE

As with so many seemingly simple things, decent tomato sauce is easy to make, but good tomato sauce is not. I thought I could make good tomato sauce until I started working at The River Café, where I met a guy called Joseph Travelli. Everyone called him "Steam Train" Travelli, because he was well known for zipping around corners, a dangerous habit in any kitchen. I came to know him best for his knack with tomato sauce. His tasted so much better than mine that I quickly realized I was still at square one, and I decided to try to crack the code on Travelli's method. Lucky me, I got to watch him make tomato sauce again and again. As far as I could tell, the two most important components to his sauce were the tomatoes and the garlic. The tomatoes must be top-quality, whether you're using fresh or canned. The better they are, the better the result. That's obvious. Not so obvious is the role of garlic. Steam Train might not have known how to turn a corner with grace, but he had a way with garlic. He browned it just enough to bring out the most warmth and umami, which would permeate the tomatoes and turn the sauce into something special. I follow his lead here, paying particularly close attention to the sizzling garlic. And since this is a book on veg, I figured that I should leave out the guanciale that adds a porky, funky flavor to some of my favorite tomato sauces. Instead, I use red onions, which give the sauce a meatiness that regular onions don't.

Working with one at a time, hold the tomatoes over a bowl and use a finger to poke through the flesh and squeeze gently so the liquid inside spills into the bowl. Strain and reserve the liquid and roughly chop the tomatoes.

Heat 3 tablespoons of the oil in a medium pot over medium-high heat until it shimmers. Add the onion and 1 teaspoon of the salt. Lower the heat to medium and cook the onions at a steady sizzle, stirring occasionally, until they go translucent, 4 to 5 minutes.

makes about 2 cups

2 cans (28 ounces each) whole tomatoes, drained and trimmed (see page 16)

4 tablespoons extra-virgin olive oil

1 medium red onion (about ½ pound), finely diced

1½ teaspoons Maldon or another flaky sea salt

2 medium garlic cloves, thinly sliced

A five-finger pinch of basil leaves, roughly chopped at the last minute

Push the onion to one side of the pot and add the garlic to the oil. Pay especially close attention to the garlic as you cook, stirring the garlic occasionally but not the onion, until the slices turn a light golden color and smell toasty, about 3 minutes. Stir it all together with the onion and cook, stirring now and then, until the slices turn golden with slightly darker edges, about 5 minutes more. Just when you start to freak out that the edges might begin to burn, stir in the tomatoes (not the liquid just yet).

Raise the heat to medium-high, and let the mixture simmer rapidly, stirring and breaking up the tomatoes a bit, until it looks less like separate bits and more like one sauce, about 3 minutes. Add the tomato liquid, bring it to a vigorous simmer, then lower the heat to maintain a gentle simmer. Cook, stirring now and then, until the sauce thickens slightly and the flavors have a chance to mingle, about 30 minutes.

Stir in the basil, the remaining 1 tablespoon of oil, and the remaining ½ teaspoon of salt. Raise the heat to bring the sauce to a proper simmer and cook until it thickens slightly and you can taste the basil a bit more, about 5 minutes.

Use the sauce right away or let it cool and store it in an airtight container in the fridge for up to 3 days.

SIMPLE BEANS

It's always nice to have dried beans in your cupboard. Even better is having cooked beans in your fridge, swimming in an earthy, olive-oil-enriched liquor. That way you're always that much closer to a hearty supper, whether you're making Bean and Mushroom Salad (page 92) or Summery Ribollita (page 110), or if you want to turn a simple vegetable dish into a satisfying meal. I like to blend some of the beans with the cooking liquid so the liquor has a little extra body and flavor. This liquor, by the way, is great in soups as a sort of vegetarian stock.

Put the beans in a medium pot with the garlic, oil, and enough water to cover them by an inch or so. Set the pot over medium-high heat and bring the liquid to a simmer. Lower the heat to maintain a gentle simmer and cook until the beans are tender and almost creamy inside but before they start bursting, 1 to 2 hours, depending on the freshness of your beans. Stir in the salt, turn off the heat, and let the beans sit for about 15 minutes in the liquid until they're fully creamy.

Fish out the garlic cloves and add them to a blender along with a few cups of the cooking liquid and a heaping cup of the beans. Blend until smooth, pour the mixture into the pot, and have a gentle stir. The beans keep in their liquid in the fridge for several days.

makes about 6 cups cooked beans and about 7 cups tasty liquid

1 pound high-quality dried borlotti, cannellini, or similar beans (about 2⅔ cups), picked over, soaked overnight in water, and drained

1 large head garlic, cloves separated and peeled

½ cup extra-virgin olive oil

1 tablespoon plus 1 teaspoon Maldon or another flaky sea salt

SIMPLE CHICKEN STOCK

I don't like to think of meat and vegetables as playing for two separate teams. They're more like good friends, each helping out the other on occasion. That's why I put a recipe for chicken stock in a book on veg. It provides a unique richness and depth to Potato Soup with Garlic and Parsley (page 62), Spring Egg Drop Soup (page 38), and Braised Peas and Little Gem Lettuce (page 24). Even though all three dishes remain focused on the flavor of vegetables, none would be as tasty without the stock in the background. Now and then as it bubbles away, I like to fish out bits of meat from the crannies of the bones, sprinkle on a little salt, and have a nibble. Even though making stock doesn't take much work, you still deserve a reward.

Put all the ingredients in a large pot and bring to a vigorous simmer over high heat. Don't let it boil or you'll end up with a cloudy stock. Reduce the heat so the water simmers only very gently and cook, skimming the gunk off the surface but resisting the urge to stir, for about 4 hours. Along the way, tweak the heat if you need to, so little bubbles just break the surface here and there. After 4 hours or so it should be ready, but give it a taste—you want it to taste like chicken. If it doesn't, let it simmer a bit longer. Once it's good and tasty, strain the stock through a fine-mesh sieve into a large pot or bowl and discard the solids.

If you mean to use the stock straightaway, skim off the clear fat with a spoon. If not, let the stock come to room temperature, then cover and chill the stock until the fat rises to the surface and solidifies. Scrape off the white fat and keep the stock in the refrigerator for up to 3 days or in the freezer for up to a month.

makes about 3 quarts

5 pounds chicken bones, such as backs, wings, and necks, cut into big chunks by your butcher

1 large Spanish onion (about 1 pound), peeled and quartered

1 medium carrot, peeled, topped, tailed, and halved lengthwise

3 medium celery stalks, halved crosswise

1 garlic head, unpeeled and halved crosswise

20 or so black peppercorns

2 small fresh bay leaves

1 small thyme sprig

4 quarts water

CARAMEL POPCORN WITH NUTS

A fantastic topping for Sweet Corn Ice Cream (page 213), this caramel corn also makes for great snacking. Fair warning: It's dangerous, this stuff. If the crunchy, sweet, salty mixture is within 50 feet, I'm drawn to it like a pig to mud.

Besides the pleasure of munching each handful, making the popcorn is silly fun: In case you forgot, it's just about the coolest thing ever. In go the golden kernels, then after a ruckus under the lid, out comes fluffy white popped corn. You can buy popping corn any time of year, though in the dead of winter, spotting a bag of kernels on a farmer's table makes for an extra-bright spot in a dark time. Even the most humble vegetables, in the most barren of seasons, can bring a bit of magic.

Position a rack in the center of the oven and preheat to 300°F. Line a baking sheet with parchment paper.

Spread the nuts on the baking sheet and bake, stirring occasionally, until the nuts are a shade or two darker and very aromatic, about 15 minutes. Transfer the nuts to a large mixing bowl and loosely cover with foil to keep warm. Leave the oven on and the parchment on the baking sheet.

Add the oil to a heavy pot large enough to hold about 8 cups of popped popcorn. Heat the oil over medium-high heat until it begins to smoke. Add the kernels and cover the pot. Once you hear the first kernels pop, position the lid so some air can escape and steady it with one hand, and with the other shake the pot vigorously until the pops are about 2 seconds apart. Put the popcorn in the bowl with the nuts and keep in a warm place, such as near the oven.

Combine the brown sugar, maple syrup, corn syrup, and butter in a medium saucepan. Attach a candy thermometer and bring the mixture to a vigorous simmer over medium-high heat. Let it simmer, without stirring, until the mixture reaches 240°F. Add the salt, vanilla

makes about 10 cups

SPECIAL EQUIPMENT
A candy thermometer

½ cup unsalted roasted peanuts

½ cup pecan halves

¼ cup blanched hazelnuts

1 tablespoon neutral oil, such as canola or grapeseed

⅓ cup popcorn kernels

½ cup packed light brown sugar

¼ cup plus 2 tablespoons pure maple syrup

¼ cup plus 2 tablespoons light corn syrup

4 tablespoons (½ stick) unsalted butter

1½ teaspoons kosher salt

½ teaspoon vanilla extract

⅛ teaspoon baking soda

extract, and baking soda and have one good stir. The mixture will froth. Immediately pour it over the popcorn and nuts, and stir to coat everything well.

Spread the mixture in an even layer onto the parchment-lined baking sheet. Pop it in the oven and bake, stirring occasionally, until the popcorn is barely sticky to the touch and crunchy, about 30 minutes. Let it cool to room temperature and break up the clusters a bit, if you'd like.

It keeps in an airtight container at room temperature for up to 3 days.

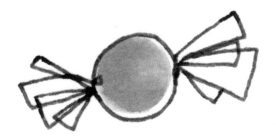

index

NOTE: Page references in *italics* refer to photos.

about the author

APRIL BLOOMFIELD is the executive chef and co-owner of the Michelin-starred The Spotted Pig, The Breslin, The John Dory, Tosca, and Salvation Taco restaurants. She won the 2014 James Beard Award for Best Chef in New York and was nominated for an Emmy for cohosting the second season of the PBS show *Mind of a Chef*. A native of Birmingham, England, she lives in New York City.

thank you